CLEAN PLATES

Manhattan 2014

A Guide to the
Healthiest Tastiest
and Most Sustainable
Restaurants for Vegetarians
and Carnivores

By JARED KOCH

Reviews by ALEX VAN BUREN

and SARAH AMANDOLARE, TALIA BERMAN, JESSICA COLLEY,
JACLYN EINIS, ALLIX GENESLAW, CHELSEA GRANT,
SCARLETT LINDEMAN, ANDREA LYNN, MEGAN MURPHY,
LISA LEEKING RUVALCABA, AMY SUNG

DISCLAIMER: I am not a medical doctor, and nothing in this book is intended to diagnose, treat or cure any medical condition, illness or disease. Anyone with a specific medical condition should consult a physician.

Published by Clean Plates
Fort Lee, NJ

Cover design by Jessica Arana
Interior design by Gary Robbins

Printed in Canada

10 9 8 7 6 5 4 3 2 1

*Library of Congress
Cataloging-in-Publication Data:*

Koch, Jared.
    Clean Plates Manhattan : a guide
    to the healthiest tastiest and most
    sustainable restaurants in Manhattan
    for vegetarians and carnivores / by Jared
    Koch ; with reviews by Alex Van Buren et.
    al. – Fort Lee, NJ : Clean Plates, 2013.
    p.   cm.
    ISBN 978-0-9859221-6-0
    1.   Food—Popular works.
    2.   Diet—Popular works.
    3.   Nutrition—Popular works.
    4.   Restaurants—New York (State)
        —New York.
    I.   Title.
    II. Van Buren, Alex.
TX355.K63   2013
641—dc22
2008940260

CONTENTS

DESIGN YOUR OWN DIET

THE RESTAURANTS

ACKNOWLEDGMENTS

My deepest gratitude, appreciation and respect to the following people, without whom this book would not exist:

To all the chefs and restaurant owners dedicated to serving delicious but healthier food. A special thanks to Dan Barber, Bill Telepan, Sarma Melngailis, Debbie Covenagh, Amy Chaplin, Rene Duran, Melissa O'Donnell and Michael Anthony for taking the time to be interviewed.

Alex Van Buren for her talents, integrity and great dinner conversation. Angela Starks and Bunny Wong for all their help writing and editing the nutritional content. Talia Berman, Andrea Lynn, Lisa LeeKing Ruvalcaba, Megan Murphy, Jessica Colley, Sarah Amandolare, Jaclyn Einis, Amy Sung, Allix Geneslaw, Scarlett Lindeman and Chelsea Grant for writing great reviews.

Jessica Arana for designing the logo and the book cover. Gary Robbins for interior design and layout. The whole gang at Monaco Lange for all of their invaluable suggestions.

Special thanks to Blake Appleby for always supporting, encouraging and inspiring me and offering her insightful opinions. To all my family, friends, teachers and clients who have contributed and enriched my life in so many significant ways. Greg Monaco for his talents, perspective and calm demeanor and for his invaluable advice every step of the way.

Maji Chien, Niles Brooks Leuthold, Laura Mordas-Schenkein, Chris Cavanagh and Ashley Spivak for all of their invaluable help and dedication.

And to Mat Zucker, Lynnda Pollio, Yvonne Roehler at Jenkins Group, Kate Basrat, Ameet Maturu, Susan Banzon, Amy Bush, Angela Davis, Chad Thompson, Sam Rosen at ThoughtLead, Peter Horjus, Vera Svezia, Barry Flemming, Jeremy Funston, Lisa Vasher, Catherine Cusamano, Mark Sclafani, Katherine Jamieson, Kathleen Spinelli, Erin Turner, Michael Ellisberg, Nancy Weiser, Carey Peters, Brett Lavender, Cassandra Caffaltas, Kim Blozie, Chelsea Holmes, Elizabeth O'Riordan, Robert John Scott, Nathan Jones and especially Andrew Cohen and everyone at EnlightenNext.

A NOTE FROM JARED

WELCOME TO CLEAN PLATES MANHATTAN 2014. For those of you already familiar with *Clean Plates*, I'd like to point out a few of our most critical updates. In addition to the reviews contributed by Alex Van Buren (my co-author and sole food critic for the original *Clean Plates Manhattan* in 2009), you'll see contributions from several other very talented food critics: Scarlett Lindeman, Allix Geneslaw, Talia Berman, Lisa LeeKing Ruvalcaba, Andrea Lynn, Megan Murphy, Jessica Colley, Sarah Amandolare, Jaclyn Einis, Amy Sung and Chelsea Grant. They have contributed over 50 new reviews of *Clean Plates*-approved eateries, making *Clean Plates Manhattan* the most comprehensive and up-to-date list of the healthiest, tastiest, and most sustainable restaurants in Manhattan.

If this is your first experience with *Clean Plates*, I welcome you! Read on to learn more.

Eating healthier does not have to be challenging. Especially in Manhattan. Especially with this book. In fact, it can be an easy, pleasurable and sacrifice-free adventure. I've created this book for you—for New Yorkers and for visitors to this great city—with exactly that in mind.

Let's face it: We dine out a lot. And restaurants can be bad-eating minefields. But they don't have to be. Who would say no if a delicious antibiotic- and hormone-free steak or a plate of tasty organic vegetables materialized in front of them? No one actually *wants* to consume hormones, antibiotics or pesticides. It's just that searching for the good stuff takes time. Fortunately, it's been done for you, and with a one-two punch: every featured selection in *Clean Plates Manhattan* is a restaurant that offers both delicious *and* nutritious fare. Rest assured because all were personally visited and screened by myself, a nutritional consultant, along with one of our talented food critics.

This book is about helping you make better, more informed choices. In fact, it's my intention that you actually will *crave* healthier food after reading it. You'll learn that there's more than one right way to eat—a theory called bio-individuality (Makes sense, right? After all, do you wear the same clothes as all of your friends? Why should food be any different?). Sure, there's a lot of nutritional information out there, but talk about confusing. That's why this guide provides an easy-to-follow education about the most important foods you will encounter when dining out. That way, you can use your knowledge to implement the life-changing diet that's right for *you*.

---

3 WAYS YOU CAN USE THIS BOOK

- To find healthy, tasty and sustainable restaurants in Manhattan.
- To learn how to change your eating habits when you dine out—and in.
- To transform your life by seeing how eating healthier can be pleasurable and startlingly simple.

By now you're probably asking yourself: Who *is* this guy? Why should I listen to anything he says? Well, honestly, I'm not that different from you. I want to be healthy so I can enjoy my life and contribute to making the world a better place. Rather than bore you with a long report about my life (you can learn more by visiting cleanplates.com), I'll touch on a few highlights for your peace of mind.

After deferring my acceptance to medical school for a decade-long stint as a successful entrepreneur, I decided that I needed to figure out my health and happiness. As part of that journey, I not only became a certified nutritional consultant, yoga instructor and health coach but also healed myself from chronic irritable bowel syndrome (IBS), fatigue and skin issues. I'm now a nutritional consultant backed by eight years of immersing myself in the formal study of nutrition— and five years of working with clients. I've had some amazing teachers: Andrew Weil, M.D., Deepak Chopra and Walter Willett, the head of nutrition at Harvard, in addition to many experts in the fields of Raw Foods, Chinese Medicine, Ayurveda, Macrobiotics, Vegetarianism and High-Protein Diets.

For my clients, and in this book, I synthesize those dietary theories in an easy-to-use format—always keeping an open mind to discovering the truth about what actually works for each individual. Thanks to my experiences, I've had several insights over the years about how we eat, all of which I will be sharing in more detail in *Clean Plates Manhattan*:

* Eating well is the easiest and best way (along with exercise and perhaps meditation) to positively affect your health and improve your quality of life.

* Contrary to conventional wisdom, healthy eating can be enjoyable and satisfying, free from the typical guilt and confusion we usually feel in relation to our food.

* No single way of eating works for everyone, but there is a healthy way to eat that's just right for *you* and *your* body.

* A quick way to upgrade your well-being: Select higher-quality, better-sourced versions of whatever foods you're currently consuming, especially when it comes to animal-based products.

* To increase nutrient intake and boost immunity, start with food that's fresh (locally grown), non-toxic (organic) and mostly plant-based (more vegetables, fruits, nuts and seeds). Think of it as a tasty trio—local, non-toxic plants.

* Reducing your intake of artificial, chemical-laden processed foods, as well as sugar, caffeine and alcohol, will have you feeling better immediately.

* Making small improvements over time leads to significant change.

* What's good for you is usually good for the environment. Growing food locally means less energy consumption. Organic items don't poison the earth. And a reduction in the demand for livestock frees up vital resources.

* It's entirely possible to commit to values of health and conscious consumerism *and* fully enjoy the pleasures of life and this wonderful city. Why? Because, increasingly, tasty and healthy food is accessible to everyone from vegans to carnivores.

One of the major reasons I wrote this book is that there's a real lack of helpful, well-organized information for people who wish to dine out mindfully and still enjoy the experience of eating. Sure, cooking at home is important and many nutrition books offer delicious recipes, but the truth is, we New Yorkers eat out a lot—it is part of the culture. Our city boasts amazing chefs and a stunning variety of cuisines; if you live here, it's likely that restaurants are where you get a huge proportion of your nourishment. During my preliminary investigations, I noted a few gaps in the advice offered by other books and websites: 1) It's easy to find places that list vegan and vegetarian establishments—but none adequately distinguish which spots are healthy (not all are) or which would be appealing for non-vegetarians. 2) Few are dedicated to omnivores who would like to frequent places that serve organic, local and sustainably-raised animal products, and those that do exist tend to be confusing, poorly researched, and neither comprehensive, nor screened for taste. That's why I created *Clean Plates* to be the most exceptionally well-researched, comprehensive and easy-to-use guide that exists; I'm certain it will help you navigate the ever-expanding maze of Manhattan's healthiest, tastiest and most sustainable restaurants.

The main inspiration for this book, however, grew out of my interactions with my clients. Several years ago, I began researching "healthy restaurants" because I believed that I could both eat healthier and enjoy the pleasures and diversity of this wonderful city. As I shared my ever-growing list of healthier restaurants with my clients, they actually started implementing changes and feeling better—a fact that inspired me to thoroughly expand my research, hire an amazing food critic, and set out to create *Clean Plates*. I learned from counseling clients that real change calls for practical tools. I think of this book as one of those significant tools.

This project is an extension of the work that I do with my clients: a way to reach more people and contribute to a growing awareness of healthy, responsible and sustainable eating. Together, let's shatter the myth that healthier eating is a sacrifice and prove that we can do it without the guilt, inconvenience, boredom and sheer lack of long-term success that characterize the usual diets.

You see, eating clean food is admirable, but I am equally interested in clean plates—the kind of food that makes you want to lick your dishes.

In good health,

Jared Koch

HOW TO USE THIS BOOK

JUST AS THERE'S NO one-size-fits-all diet for everyone, there's no one right way to read and use this book. But I'd like to point out several helpful features.

Take It With You Everywhere

Constructed to be small and lightweight, *Clean Plates Manhattan* is easy to slip in a bag or back pocket, and its rounded corners will keep it from getting dog-eared. No matter where you are in Manhattan, you'll be able to quickly locate a restaurant that serves a healthy, delicious version of the cuisine you're in the mood for—from fast food to fine dining, vegan to omnivore and any combination thereof. Don't want to keep it on you? Another option is to store one at home and one at the office (hey, I won't stop you from buying two—the price has been kept low to make the book accessible to as many people as possible).

Learn More About Healthier Eating

Take a peek at the sections of the book preceding the restaurant reviews, where I lay out my *Five Precepts for Eating Well*. In those sections I provide an easy-to-follow education on the pros and cons of all the different foods you're likely to encounter at restaurants. From beef to milk to cheese to less-known items like kefir, I've got you covered. Due to the guide's size and scope, it's not a comprehensive list or discussion but rather a very strong foundation from which you can make intelligent and informed choices. Armed with my *Five Precepts* and a clear understanding of different foods, you'll be able to implement healthier eating habits immediately.

Find the Healthy Restaurant You Want with Easy-to-Use Listings

I don't want anyone to be left out. So whether you're a vegetarian, vegan or meat-eater—and whether you want to spend lavishly or lightly—I've tracked down restaurants for you (always serving delicious meals, naturally). *Clean Plates Manhattan* boasts an incredibly diverse array of over 100 establishments (including full reviews) representing all manner of cuisines, budgets and geographic locations. Among many other options, you'll find (a) the best-tasting hormone and antibiotic-free animal products; (b) the best-tasting, high-quality vegetarian dishes; and (c) the best-tasting naturally sweetened desserts.

Find a Restaurant Quickly Using the Index
The index offers a way to quickly reference what you are looking for in a variety of different configurations from geography to brunch options to top date spots.

Discover How Eating Well Can Be Fun, Guilt-Free and Life-Changing
I like to think of this book as a tool. It gives you the information you need to eat healthier—with little effort, since the book does the work for you—and puts to rest the excuse that healthy foods are too inaccessible and expensive to incorporate into your life. And then there's the domino effect: when you crave better food and eat more of it, your body responds, rewarding you with better moods, energy and health.

Save the World While You're At It
As a nutritional consultant and health coach, I believe in caring for the world around you—an attitude that can become the impetus for environmentally beneficial actions like selecting organic, local food.

Get Fed by Clean Plates

 Download our free companion iPhone App

Visit www.cleanplates.com to sign up for our free email newsletter, full of restaurant news, healthy eating tips, recipes and more!

RESTAURANT REVIEW PROCESS AND CRITERIA

THIS BOOK IS MEANT to be an indispensable resource for your real-life needs: it's practical, easy to use, easy to follow...and life changing. Yes, life changing. Because if you start eating at several of the restaurants we recommend, I can almost guarantee that you'll feel better, become healthier and begin to crave food that's good for you.

Maybe you're a vegetarian with a meat-eating, foodie spouse. Or a workaholic who orders in takeout at the office. Or perhaps you're both. No matter what, this book features a restaurant for you. In fact it has a restaurant for nearly every permutation of taste, cuisine and geographic preference: upscale and fast food, East Village and Midtown East, Korean and Italian, vegetarian, vegan, meat-serving and much more.

There are only two constants. Every single featured restaurant serves *delicious* and *nutritious* dishes. How'd we find them? In the next several paragraphs, I explain.

Why We Used a Food Critic and a Nutritionist

Eating healthy foods is considerably more appealing when you enjoy what you're eating, yet most health-food guides give scant attention to taste. Not this one. This one should please the most critical, severe and discerning of foodies. How can I be sure? Well, after interviewing several seasoned writers, I initially selected and worked with Alex Van Buren, a former *Time Out New York* food writer and *Martha Stewart Living* research editor. As more New York restaurants embraced healthy and sustainable practices, I brought on the equally talented Scarlett Lindeman, Allix Geneslaw, Talia Berman, Lisa LeeKing Ruvalcaba, Andrea Lynn, Chelsea Grant, Jaclyn Einis, Megan Murphy, Jessica Colley, Sarah Amandolare and Amy Sung to sift through the new potential contenders (for bios of each of our writers, visit www. cleanplates.com). Each critic and I had to agree on every restaurant as far as taste goes; if she or I didn't think it served delicious food, it didn't make it into this book. And as a nutritional consultant, I screened and approved every spot to make sure its meals were healthy. How can you be certain you're going to get a healthy *and* delicious meal? Just eat at any of the restaurants featured in *Clean Plates Manhattan*.

How We Found the Restaurants

My goal was to compile a list of healthy Manhattan restaurants that accommodated both vegetarians and carnivores and was as wide-ranging as possible. From there, the food critics and I would whittle it down to the very best. I already had a small file of such establishments, assembled over the years; I added to it by tracking down healthy eateries in every way possible. I read other guidebooks, searched online, asked restaurant owners, petitioned my friends and literally walked and drove around the city looking for places. The result: a master list of a couple hundred restaurants. True, I may have missed a few—this is Manhattan, after all, home to a dizzying array of eateries; plus, before now, there hasn't been a good resource for vegetarians and especially carnivores seeking healthy but tasty foods. In fact, that's one of the reasons why I also set up a website (cleanplates.com) where you can stay up-to-date, share your opinions, and give and receive information about closings and openings.

The Screening, Researching, Reviewing and Fact-Checking Process

First, I subjected each place on our master list of several hundred restaurants to a health-screening process. Posing as a potential customer over the phone, the *Clean Plates* team and I queried the staff about their preparation and sourcing methods (examples: Is your meat hormone- and antibiotic-free? Is it grass-fed? What is your apple pie sweetened with? Do you use a microwave?). In addition, I thoroughly reviewed the menu online or in person.

If the restaurant passed this initial health test, a food critic and I visited it incognito (so that we wouldn't receive special treatment). We ordered as wide a variety of foods as possible—appetizers, side dishes, main courses and desserts—and didn't just stick to our own tastes. In addition, we asked the staff more questions, some a repeat of what we had asked on the phone (more examples: Is your water filtered? Is your produce local and organic?).

Next, the food critic and I discussed whether the restaurant met our taste and health criteria; again, we had to agree as far as taste goes. After we selected a restaurant, I or someone on my team sent a detailed survey to the owner, manager or chef to learn more about their vendors and sourcing and to ensure they answered our initial queries honestly.

Our Criteria

We struggled between being selective and comprehensive and, in the end, decided it was important to offer a hybrid of both. When choosing a restaurant, we took the following areas into consideration:

- Taste
- Atmosphere
- Type of cuisine: We wanted to make sure a wide variety of cuisines were included, from pizza and burgers to Indian and French foods, and on and on. And we added extra points for accessibility, such as when a vegetarian restaurant had a menu that most carnivores would enjoy or when a carnivore-friendly place offered several vegetarian options.
- Lifestyle: To ensure that personal tastes and needs were met, we included casual, power lunch, and fine dining establishments, as well as those that are family-friendly and date-worthy—and more. Even if you occasionally crave fast-food, we have you covered (and that's *healthier* fast-food, naturally).
- Geography: Wherever you find yourself in Manhattan—wherever you live, work, shop and hang out—we've identified a restaurant nearby that serves healthy and delicious meals.
- Healthfulness of ingredients: All of our restaurants that serve animal products source, at the very least, almost entirely (if not entirely) from farms raising animals without the use of hormones or

antibiotics.

In addition, we awarded points for restaurants that:

- Source grass-fed, organic, free-range animals
- Order from small, local farms
- Include a high percentage of vegetables on the menu
- Purchase produce from organic or local purveyors
- Filter their water
- Use high-quality salts
- Offer naturally sweetened desserts
- Include organic and biodynamic wines and organic coffees on their menu
- Sell better quality soda and soft drinks
- Have wheat- and gluten-free options

We deducted points from restaurants that:

- Offer animal foods that weren't sustainably raised
- Use too many fake soy products
- Have too much seitan, a wheat-gluten product used as a fake-meat substitute
- Don't include enough vegetable options or greens on the menu
- Follow poor-quality cooking methods, such as frying
- Cook with poor-quality oils
- Overemphasize dairy, shellfish, veal and foie gras

Our Featured Selections: Clean Plates Approved!

In alphabetical order, the best restaurants (over 100)—the places that passed our taste and health tests with very high scores—are given informative and entertaining reviews by one of our food critics. For easier browsing, we include icons that provide key information (Is it vegetarian? Does it serve animal foods? Is it a good budget pick?).

If you simply stick to eating at a combination of these restaurants when you dine out, there's a good chance that you'll improve your quality of life and your health. Why? Well, for one thing, you'll be putting better foods into your body, and it will respond in kind. For another, you'll start to associate delicious meals with healthy meals—and you'll begin to crave the latter. In fact, consuming junk food will seem less and less appealing. And you'll be doing all of this with little effort because the restaurants—and this book—will have done the work for you. All you have to do is eat!

Visit Cleanplates.com

In addition to the restaurants featured in this book, on our website we include what I like to call the Honorable Mentions: restaurants that didn't quite meet all of our criteria but still do a better than average job using healthier and more sustainable ingredients. Our online database rates these "Honorable Mentions" to give you an idea as to how discerning you need to be at each establishment. Additionally, by visiting cleanplates.com you can sign up for our daily email which feeds you some of the best nutritional tips, recipes and behind the scenes looks at your favorite *Clean Plates* establishments and chefs.

Other great reasons to visit cleanplates.com:
- Sign up for updates on new restaurant openings and closings
- Get notified of restaurant promotions and offerings
- Read interviews with health-conscious and sustainable-savvy chefs
- Browse menus
- Order delivery via SeamlessWeb
- Reserve a table through OpenTable
- Stay informed with healthier eating tips and the latest in nutrition and sustainable food news
- Follow us on Twitter and "like" us on Facebook.
- Learn more about the *Clean Plates* mobile version.
- Learn more about the *Clean Plates Cookbook*.

WHY EAT HEALTHIER?

For Physical Health and Quality of Life

FINANCIAL COLUMNISTS LIKE TO point out that ordering a $3 latte every day adds up to $1,000 a year that otherwise would have been accruing interest in a CD. Our daily food choices operate according to similar principles; instead of building up our financial assets, however, we are building our health resources.

Several cases in point: You wake up, yawning, get dressed, and (a) start the day with a cup of herbal tea or glass of water with lemon to accompany your bowl of oatmeal and fruit; or (b) pick up a Starbucks coffee with sugar on your way to work, skipping breakfast. Later the same day, you and your co-workers order out for (a) wild salmon with vegetables and brown rice; or (b) fast-food hamburgers and fries. You get the picture: Going for the "b" option day in and day out adds up to nothing good, while repeated "a" choices equals a lifetime of overall optimal well-being.

That's why we should remind ourselves why it's worth it to be healthy (typically, better looks, lower weight!). But how about more energy, feeling better, lower healthcare bills, and even better sex. So think about those benefits the next time you're tempted by the often-insidious forces that affect our food choices, like instant gratification, biochemical addiction, emotional and peer pressure, and just plain old habit.

Our health may be affected more by the foods we eat than by any other factor. I think that's great news, since it means we can do something about it. Of course, exercise, sleep and genetics—not to mention our relationships, career and spirituality—count, too. But the reason "you are what you eat" has endured as a phrase is because what we consume builds, fuels, cleanses or—unfortunately—pollutes our very cells.

At the end of the day, it all comes down to choices.

For the World Beyond Your Plate

Here's a new one: an organic apple a day keeps the greenhouse gases away. Translation? Eating naturally is good for nature. It's not only physical health that inspires me to be conscious about what I eat—it's also the environment. Here's a list of simple ways to positively affect the planet through your food choices.

1. CUT DOWN ON ANIMAL PRODUCTS.

No need to go vegetarian to reduce your impact. But consuming less meat—poultry, beef, fish, dairy and eggs—is a powerful way to help the earth. I hope the following facts motivate you to skip a main course of meat or dine at a vegetarian restaurant now and then, even if you're an omnivore.

- Wasted water. Beef is one of the worst offenders; its production in the United States alone requires more water than growing the world's fruit and vegetable crop.
- Wasted land. Livestock consume grain that uses up many acres.
- Wasted energy. It takes ten times more fossil fuel to produce a meat-based diet than a plant-based one. That statistic led the United Nations to declare "Raising animals for food generates more greenhouse gases than all the cars and trucks in the world combined."

- Wasted, er, waste. Don't picture this while you're eating, but imagine the amount of sewage generated by farm animals, which comprise three times the number of humans on the planet.

2. STOCK UP ON ORGANIC FOODS.

More toxic than ever before, pesticides and herbicides contaminate the soil, water and air which in turn poison both humans and wildlife. So support restaurants that source organic products or suggest that your favorite local eatery consider purchasing from Certified Naturally Grown Farms (certifiednaturallygrown.org), an organization that exceeds USDA organic standards and is locally based in upstate New York.

> **TIP: A WORD OF CAUTION**
>
> Just because locally grown and organic foods are better for the environment doesn't mean they're always healthier for our bodies. Locally grown organic sugar? Sorry, still sugar to your body.

3. GO YIMBY (YES IN MY BACKYARD) BY CHOOSING LOCALLY GROWN FOODS.

Most food travels from the farm to the restaurant on a long-distance trek, gobbling up fuel and requiring environmentally damaging packaging. As Stephen Hopp says in his wife Barbara Kingsolver's book *Animal, Vegetable, Miracle*, "If every U.S. citizen ate just one meal a week composed of locally and organically raised meats and produce, we would reduce our country's oil consumption by over 1.1 million barrels of oil every week."

4. AVOID GMOS.

The name certainly doesn't sound healthy: genetically modified organisms, aka GMOs. These artificially altered crops require an enormous amount of pesticides (they even produce pesticides within their own cells), and they cross-contaminate other crops and harm wildlife. The majority of soy (as in tofu), corn and canola crops are now GMO plants; if these items are staples in your diet, frequent eateries that serve organic versions.

5. SAY SAYONARA TO BOTTLED WATER.

Americans use two million plastic bottles *every five minutes*. Imagine them all stacked up in a pile. The amount of oil needed to make those bottles equals about 15 million barrels a year. Even recycling them means using more fossil fuels. Opt for filtered water when available and encourage restaurant owners to invest in a filtration system.

WHAT'S MORE IMPORTANT: LOCALLY GROWN OR ORGANIC?

Organic but non-local produce is free of pesticides harmful to our bodies and the soil but requires extra energy to travel from farm to table and loses nutrients along the way. *Locally Grown* but non-organic goods retain most of their nutrients because of the speed at which they get to our plates, but they may be sprayed with chemicals, which are damaging to our bodies, the soil and the atmosphere. *The answer:* Unfortunately, if you can't get an item locally grown and organic, there is no easy answer. It is a matter of personal choice and if you choose one or the other you are doing pretty good.

DESIGN YOUR OWN DIET

I BELIEVE THERE *IS* a dream diet for everyone—it's just not the same for each person. That brings me to a key principle of this book:

THE FIRST PRECEPT: There's more than one right way to eat.

As nutrition pioneer Roger Williams writes in his groundbreaking 1950s book *Biochemical Individuality*, "If we continue to try to solve problems on the basis of the average man, we will be continually in a muddle. Such a man does not exist."

We're all biochemically—genetically, hormonally and so on—different, and the idea that this should guide our eating habits has recently begun to excite the leading-edge medical and nutrition community. Experts are beginning to talk about the benefits of individualizing our diets rather than giving advice based on recommended daily allowances (RDA) or the United States Department of Agriculture's (USDA'S) "My Plate", both created with the "average" person in mind.

How We Differ

As you read through my list of how we're all unique, some of the points may seem obvious (of course someone training for a marathon requires different foods than someone sitting in front of a computer all day, for instance). But part of what I'd like to get across is that these distinctions manifest themselves not only between individuals, but also between your different selves—your tired self, your active self and the like. The key is to pay attention to how your body reacts to various foods and to what it's telling you at any given moment.

- Genetic Makeup: To a large extent, the anatomy and body chemistry that you inherited from your ancestors determine your nutritional needs and ability to benefit from particular foods. For example, a few recent studies have shown that some people possess the genetic ability to metabolize caffeine more efficiently than others. Research has also revealed that specific groups of people have the genetic makeup to absorb vitamin B12 with ease, or benefit greatly from broccoli's cancer-fighting nutrients—while others lack those genes.

- Culture and Background: Your ethnicity and upbringing influence how your body acts. For instance, several of my friends have inherited a genetic ability enabling them to drink milk, but my friend who is Asian is lactose intolerant, as are many of his compatriots—his grandparents came to America from a country where milk rarely makes it onto the menu. So it's helpful to consider which foods are part of your culture and background, and incorporate the appropriate ones into your diet.
- Lifestyle: A man training for a marathon requires different foods than a person who does an hour of yoga each week.
- Day-to-day physical health: Pay attention to your physical health symptoms to figure out what foods you need. Sick? Miso soup may be just the thing. Sneezing constantly? Avoid dairy and sugar; the former causes the body to produce mucus and the latter weakens the immune system.
- Gender: Whether you're a man or a woman affects your diet needs. For example, menstruating women require more iron than men, but men need more zinc than their female counterparts to nourish their reproductive systems.
- Age: A growing, active teen will be ravenous at dinnertime; the same person, 60 years later, will likely find that his appetite is waning.
- Seasons and Climate: Even the weather affects what's best for you to eat. When it's hot outside, the body will likely crave cooling foods like salads; on a cold winter day, hot soup is more appealing.

Eating as a Bio-Individual

The philosophy that no single way of eating is right for everyone isn't new. Both Traditional Chinese Medicine and India's Ayurvedic system revolve around prescribing the most appropriate diet for specific categories of body types and constitutions.

More recent incarnations of these ancient approaches include the blood-type diet and metabolic typing. The blood-type diet was made famous a decade ago by naturopath Peter D'Adamo, who theorized (to put it very simply) that people with blood type O do best eating meat, but type A's thrive as vegetarians. The thinking behind the discovery? Type O's descended from ancient hunters while type A's came from agricultural civilizations. The idea behind metabolic typing (again, to put it simply) is that your metabolism dictates the appropriate percentage of proteins or carbohydrates in your diet; those who metabolize proteins well require extra animal foods, while others do better with more carbs.

Not everyone agrees. Proponents of *The China Study*, a 2005 book by two nutritional biochemists who conducted a 20-year survey of Chinese diets, argue that animal consumption is the leading cause of human disease, while followers of Weston A. Price, a dentist who carried out extensive health research in many countries, rely on culturally based studies to back up their claim that animal proteins and organ meats have benefits. Ultimately, the jury is still out (and probably always will be) on whether we have evolved to be omnivores or vegetarians. Though I do believe in the importance of our culture moving more toward a vegetarian-based diet, I have also observed that, while some people thrive on a vegetarian or vegan diet, others do not—some people require (high-quality) animal protein to function optimally.

HOW SHOULD YOU APPROACH OTHER DIETARY THEORIES?

One diet (it's pushing it to call it a dietary theory!) that most of us would like to move away from is the standard American diet (or SAD, as I call it). So what should we move toward? Well, we all have different needs, but that doesn't mean we have to invent diets from scratch. We have help: Other established dietary theories. It's worth knowing about them, so you can consider which parts of each work for you.

For instance, if you're energetic, enjoy a challenge and possess a strong digestive system, you fit the description of a good candidate for raw foodism. It's a relatively new diet based on ancient principles in which vegetables, fruits, nuts and seeds are served uncooked—or heated to a maximum of 118 degrees Fahrenheit in order to maintain nutrients and enzymes. Fit the description but balking at consuming only uncooked foods? Maybe partial raw foodism is right for you (say, 50 percent raw and 50 percent cooked). Or perhaps you're eager to transition away from junk food or dairy and are very disciplined and love Asian food to boot; in that case, a macrobiotic diet may be right for you. It's a route that heavily emphasizes rice, however, so it's not the best choice for someone who doesn't do well on grains. And for many people, considering vegetarianism makes sense. If you do decide to experiment with not eating meat, be sure to avoid the pitfalls that many vegans and vegetarians accidentally step into—namely, eating too many processed foods, carbohydrates, dairy and sugar, as well as consuming too much soy in the form of fake-meat products.

Still confused? Think of it as designing your own diet using bits and pieces of good, but different, ideas. The point is that you don't need to adhere to any particular theory (they all have their pros and cons and none are right for everyone). Instead, tailor what you eat to your biology, body, blood type, hormones, tastes and way of looking at the world. My next four precepts will help to guide your choices.

How We're the Same

Our food choices often become another way of separating us. When there are moral underpinnings to our choices, it's especially tempting to think that "my way is the only right way to eat." What I like most about bio-individuality is that the focus is on how our physical selves can achieve their fullest potential. In my opinion, when that happens—when we're able to thrive physically—we've created an unshakable foundation for living to our fullest potential and for making a meaningful contribution to our collective well-being as a species and a planet.

Being different should bring us together. Why? Well, partially because it's about realizing that other people have needs distinct from ours. Some types love to begin their day with a shot of wheatgrass— but perhaps the thought makes you turn green. And while your friends can't imagine living without an occasional hamburger or slice of pizza, you might thrive on hearty salads and raw foods. And we all know that irritating person who can gobble up everything in sight and remain slim—a profile that many of us don't have. Hopefully being aware of these distinctions will lead us to be less critical of others—and less likely to feel guilty about our own choices. Judgment and guilt, after all, are bad for your health. At the very least, they really mess with your digestion.

BIO-INDIVIDUALITY MEANS THAT THERE'S no perfect diet for everyone. There *is*, however, the perfect food for everyone—real food. It's what we're designed to eat, regardless of our lifestyle, genetic makeup and other differences. Which leads me to my next premise.

THE SECOND PRECEPT: The overwhelming majority of your diet should consist of natural, high-quality and whole foods.

Which means…what? What, exactly, is real food? It's a question I often get from my clients. Once upon a time, it had an obvious answer, but, over the past hundred years, food has become increasingly unlike itself: processed, altered with chemicals, dyed unnatural colors, flavored with suspect ingredients and generally turned as artificial as can be.

These kinds of changes generally result in more toxins and fewer nutrients. In my opinion, the success of diets like macrobiotics and raw foods in claiming to help heal diabetes and even cancer (according to some studies) is due in large part to the fact that both diets call for increasing your intake of real, high quality, whole foods while reducing consumption of artificial and chemical-laden dishes.

TIP: DON'T GET SIDETRACKED BY FOCUSING ONLY ON CALORIES

Many people equate reducing calories with a healthier lifestyle, but I firmly believe that the quality of the foods we eat are much more important—even when it comes to losing weight. Here's a way of looking at it: Think of food as fuel. Does a car run best on poor-quality fuel? No, of course not. And our bodies are the same: They need optimal fuel. Another way of looking at it is to ask yourself: What's better for my body—1,800 calories of junk food and candy bars, or 2,000 calories of vegetables and fruits? I think you get the idea!

All this means we desperately need to get back to basics. To help you with the terms (high quality, whole, natural) and to give you an answer to the question above (What, exactly, is real food?), read on.

Real, aka Natural

In this book, I use the terms *real* and *natural* synonymously, a fact that may help you distinguish real from artificial. Knowing what's natural is largely a matter of intuition and common sense; it's not as if you're going to start bringing a checklist to restaurants.

Nevertheless, you'll become a pro at identifying the real thing more quickly if you ask yourself a couple of questions the next time you eat. These questions include: What would I eat if I lived in the wild? What has the earth and nature provided for humans to eat? What have I, as a human, evolved to eat? To keep it simple, focus on what grows out of the ground or on a tree. In addition, think vegetables, fruits, nuts, seeds, beans, grains, herbs and animal foods.

TIP: AN EASY WAY TO FIGURE OUT IF IT'S REAL FOOD

Just ask yourself this question: Was it made in nature or in a factory? Visualize where the item began its life. Perhaps you'll see it hanging on a bush, growing on a tree, sprouting up from the earth or grazing in a field. If it's fizzing to life in a test tube, move on.

Quality

A peach from the grocery store is a real-food item—it was made in nature and wasn't flavored in a factory—but that doesn't mean it's the best quality. The more of the following qualities the peach has, the higher its quality: it's organic, with fewer chemicals and more nutrients than its non-organic counterpart; locally grown, so it requires less artificial ripening and storage and loses fewer nutrients en route from farm to plate; non-irradiated, since radiation destroys nutrients and changes an item's chemical structure; and not genetically modified (non-GMO), an unnatural process with unknown consequences.

In addition, ask yourself if additives, flavorings, coloring or preservatives were used. It's not always obvious in a restaurant, but it's worth considering. For instance, a cupcake with fire-engine red icing probably has, among other things, icing that's artificially colored.

Whole

This term is about processes and cooking methods: The fewer things done to a food, the better. Basically, cooking and preparing food makes it less whole—but that doesn't necessarily mean the dish in question is unhealthy.

Raw foods (that is, uncooked) are in their natural state with their nutrients intact. Yet cooking is often considered the first step in the digestive process. Why? Well, it breaks down the food's cell walls and fiber, making it easier to absorb the food's nutrients. Although I am not typically a proponent of a 100% Raw-Food diet, I do believe that we should aim to eat a significant amount of raw foods as well as some cooked foods. The ratio will ultimately depend on the strength of your digestive system and personal tastes.

When examining the healthfulness of a prepared dish, you should consider:

* The cooking methods used. Err on the side of undercooking, since prolonged exposure to high heat destroys nutrients, enzymes and water content. Examples: Steaming or poaching (good) versus frying (not good) or microwaving (bad).
* The wholeness of the ingredients. Examples: A bowl of berries (good) versus fruit juice with sugar (not good).
* The number of steps or processes used to make the food. Examples: A bowl of oatmeal made from whole oats (good) versus cereal made into flakes (not so good).

What to Ask

Some establishments make meals from scratch, while others pre-make recipes in bulk and microwave them on demand. To find out whether your dish is real, quality and whole, ask the staff to confirm your meal's origins, ingredients and preparation techniques.

The questions you have may include whether brown rice can be substituted for white; if the cheese is raw or pasteurized; if the cakes are made with butter (real) or margarine (fake); whether the salmon is artificially colored or is the genuine wild-harvested article; and if the beef comes from a grass-fed cow or one fattened with grains, antibiotics and growth hormones.

I also like to know if the vegetables on my plate have just been steamed or whether the only kitchen tool required was a can opener. Peas from a can, for instance, often come with added salt. The same goes for fruit. Say there's a restaurant that lists peaches and cream on the dessert menu. Are those high-quality, real peaches or the kind that come out of a can (where they've been marinating in flavored-sugar syrup)?

A Word About Beverages

And don't forget the drinks. Is the water filtered or from the city's chlorinated supply? The former is actually closer to fresh, natural water. Is the soda sweetened with fruit juice or with high-fructose corn syrup? And that coffee—decaffeinated naturally?

Think of these ideas as practice exercises for your "food radar"—a muscle of sorts that will grow stronger with use. The more you check for the differences between whole and unwholesome, high quality and run-of-the-mill, real and processed, the more automatic eating real, whole and high-quality foods will become.

Foods For Thought

Fats, sweeteners, grains, animal products: They sound like basics, but they come in many guises—and are the cause of many debates. Take bread. Mom always told you it was an essential source of fiber, but your newspaper's science section just ran an article about how humans aren't designed to eat grains. At any rate, you're not going to forswear bread completely because you love it—but should you pair it with butter or with margarine? The latter, after all, contains fewer calories. But wasn't there a television report the other day about the evils of margarine?

The fact is, confusion and controversy surround many types of food—some more than others. To clear things up and to give you the tools to design your own diet, I've compiled information about various foods and food categories, from vegetables and fruits to meat and dairy. What you learn will enable you to make smart dietary choices.

WHAT I'M ABOUT TO say might be difficult to absorb—not because you've never heard it before, but rather because you've heard it, in some form, thousands of times. But let me tell you what it is, and then I'll address figuring out how to make it stick:

THE THIRD PRECEPT: Everyone would be better off if a larger proportion of their diet consisted of plants—mostly vegetables (in particular, leafy greens), along with some nuts, seeds and fruits.

To get this message to sink in, I encourage clients to think about it in big, overarching terms. I like to point out that eating plants is a way of taking in the energy of the sun. As a life force, the sun contributes to our health and sense of well-being enormously. Without it there would be no life on earth. Want more of it? Eat more plants. They're a more direct source of "sun food" than meat; when we eat animals, we are indirectly consuming what they themselves already ate.

If this concept is a bit too esoteric, consider it from a scientific point of view. What gives green plants their color? It's chlorophyll, the pigment in leaves that enables them to absorb the sun's rays using a process called photosynthesis. Many nutritionists believe that when we eat green leaves, we take in that stored solar energy. Chlorophyll enriches blood, kills germs, detoxifies the bloodstream and liver, reduces bodily odors and controls the appetite.

Still snoozing off when you hear "eat more plants"? Maybe telling yourself, "I'll have more energy" will provide the necessary motivation instead.

To help you navigate between different types of plants, the following two sections of this book are devoted to information about vegetables and fruits. It's not wrong to eat meat—in fact, it can be healthy for certain people—but eat lots of plants, and you'll start to feel better. The next two sections show you why.

THINK ABOUT IT: YET ANOTHER REASON TO EAT VEGGIES

Have you ever heard of anyone being overweight or getting heart disease or cancer from eating too many vegetables?

Veggie Tales

Pity the unappreciated vegetable. Perpetually shunted to the side—as a garnish, appetizer, side dish—it rarely gets to give all that it has to offer. What does it offer, you ask? An enormous amount of nutrients and health-boosting properties in the form of vitamins, minerals, fiber, phytochemicals and antioxidants. Vegetables should form the bulk of your diet.

QUICK DEFINITION: ANTIOXIDANTS

Their name says it all: they're *anti*-oxidants. They counteract oxidation—and the free radicals believed to speed up aging and disease. A variety of elements cause our bodies to produce excess free radicals. Some are "bad," like toxic air and the chemicals to which we're exposed, but some are everyday, such as exercise and the normal process of metabolizing food for energy. Fortunately, you can combat these excess free radicals by eating more vegetables (as well as fruits, nuts and seeds), which are abundant in antioxidants.

If you're a vegetarian, aim to increase the proportion of veggies that you consume relative to the amount of grains, beans, dairy, sugar and tofu in your diet. Similarly, omnivores should be mindful of the meat-to-vegetable ratio in each meal.

And I'd like to take a moment to remind you about my second premise—eat high-quality, natural and whole vegetables. For one thing, they taste noticeably better. In addition, local, organic vegetables suffer less nutrient loss than their long-distance counterparts; they also reap the benefits of organic soils, which are rich in nutrients.

In addition, these do-it-all veggies possess a characteristic that many people don't know to look for but that's important for good health: they're alkalizing. In contrast, most foods in the standard American diet—especially meats, sugar and white flour—are acid-forming. Without getting into the nitty-gritty science of it, I'd like to point out that most disease states within the body occur in an acidic environment. Foods that create alkalinity are healthier.

To help you order at restaurants, here's a roundup of the types of vegetables you're likely to encounter—and how they affect your body:

LEAFY GREENS should be a priority because they're one of the most nutrient-dense foods. Chock-full of chlorophyll, they also boast a calcium-to-magnesium ratio that makes them great bone builders and encourages relaxation and appropriate nerve-and-muscle responsiveness, ensuring the body's smooth functioning. And as well as being a good way to obtain iron, vitamin C and folic acid, leafy greens contain essential amino acids, meaning they're an excellent source of protein—one that potentially rivals the kind from animals. Let's take a look at some of the more common leafy greens.

Kale, swiss chard, collards and spinach are all chef favorites. If possible, ask for yours to be lightly steamed or even served raw, both options that retain more nutrients than frying. A quick sauté with garlic is another delicious and healthy alternative.

Spinach enjoys an impressive reputation (think Popeye) but contains oxalic acid, an anti-nutrient that prevents the absorption and use of calcium and may contribute to kidney stones and gout. While some nutritional experts insist that thorough cooking neutralizes the acid, others report that overcooking makes it toxic (the latter group suggest eating it raw). Until there's a definitive answer, I recommend enjoying spinach without overdoing it, and opting instead for kale, swiss chard or collard greens when possible.

Lettuce, mesclun greens, watercress and arugula often appear in salads, meaning they're raw and still contain all their nutrients and enzymes (watercress in particular is rich in B vitamins). But skip iceberg lettuce. The most common salad green in the United States, iceberg lettuce has few nutrients and tends to be heavily sprayed.

Parsley and dandelion greens, both highly nutritious, don't make it onto menus as often as other greens; when they do, it's usually as a garnish or as part of a salad. Parsley is incredibly rich in iron and

Drinking the juice of
any type of green—not
just wheatgrass—is
a speedy way to get
a nutrient infusion
without your teeth or
digestive system having
to work at breaking
down the plants' cell
walls. Nevertheless,
don't stop eating whole
greens, since they
provide fiber as well as
some nutrients that may
be lost or oxidized in
the juicing process.

vitamin C, while bitter dandelion—an acquired taste—offers some vitamin D and helps to cleanse the liver.

Wheatgrass tends to conjure up images of earthy-crunchy types, but I think a better way to look at it is as a treat for health connoisseurs. It boasts one of the most concentrated sources of chlorophyll, a pigment (as you may recall from earlier) that captures the sun's energy and passes its healthful effects along to your body. New Yorkers knock it back like a shot of espresso at juice bars and health-food restaurants all over the city.

CRUCIFEROUS VEGETABLES are plants in the cabbage family, a category that includes broccoli, cauliflower, Brussels sprouts, kale, bok choy and all cabbages (yep, there's some overlap with the "leafy greens" group). High in vitamin C and soluble fiber, these foods also are crammed with nutrients boasting potent anti-cancer properties. And only cruciferous vegetables contain isothiocyanates, a nutrient that has been associated with a decrease in lung cancer.

These veggies crop up in all guises on menus, most often as a side (of broccoli or cauliflower, for instance), but sometimes in stir-fries and casseroles. And they're common at Asian and raw-food eateries, where items like broccoli or kale tend to be served raw and marinated—a preparation method that imparts a sautéed texture without the nutrient loss that comes with actual sautéing.

ROOT VEGETABLES include carrots, beets, potatoes, parsnips, yams, turnips and radishes, each with a unique nutritional profile. Carrots, for instance, contain the antioxidant known as betacarotene; beets, crammed with iron, enrich the blood. White potatoes, however, have more sugar and fewer nutrients than yams or sweet potatoes. When possible, inquire about substituting one of the latter two in potato-based dishes.

MUSHROOMS probably generate the most controversy of all vegetables, at least as far as their health claims go. Some nutritionists advise steering clear because they are, after all, fungus, and are therefore potentially infectious. They're also hard to digest. Other experts, however, particularly those who study Asian cultures, vaunt the medicinal properties of mushrooms. Personally, I like to stick to the shiitake and maitake (hen of the woods) varieties, both of which have cancer-fighting and immune-boosting properties (recent studies have suggested that button mushrooms contain several goodies such as antioxidants, too).

KIMCHI and **SAUERKRAUT** come in what is possibly the best form in which to consume your veggies—raw and fermented. Literally "alive," they teem with nutrients, enzymes and probiotics, which aid digestion.

As central to Korean culture as pasta is to Italy, kimchi may contain any type of vegetable but often includes cabbage and carrots, which are typically spiced up with garlic, ginger or cayenne. Because of its spiciness, kimchi makes not only a great snack, but also a delicious condiment. A German staple, sauerkraut is made from cultured cabbage. Both naturally fermented treats are becoming popular in all types of restaurants as a side dish, in sandwiches or as part of a main course.

QUICK DEFINITION: GOOD GERMS AND ENZYMES

We hear it constantly: such-and-such food boasts enzymes and probiotics. But what do those funny-sounding things do?

Enzymes control the rate of every chemical reaction in your system, which means that you need them to digest food. So what happens when we don't get our enzymes, which are potentially destroyed by overcooking? Bad digestion.

Probiotics are healthy bacteria in the gut that rid your intestines of bad stuff. The upshot? You're healthier when you get probiotics.

SEAWEEDS, which I like to think of as vegetables from the sea, include nori (used to wrap sushi), hijiki, wakame, dulse and many others. Extremely dense in minerals, they add a salty, oceanlike taste to dishes.

Asian establishments (in particular Japanese restaurants, as you can probably tell from the aforementioned names) serve seaweed often. So do vegetarian eateries. Not familiar with this food? Try a seaweed salad or ask for extra in your miso soup; both are easy, delicious ways to familiarize yourself with sea veggies—and to enjoy a big, healthy dose of minerals.

Feeling Fruity

Think of them as sweets that are good to eat: fruits are good sources of fiber, antioxidants, phytochemicals and vitamins, and provide energy via their easily digestible sugars.

They should comprise a small percentage of your overall plant intake, so it's appropriate that fruits make up a small percentage of the amount of plant food offered at restaurants—vegetables pop up all over menus, but fruits tend to appear only in juices, smoothies or desserts.

> **QUICK DEFINITION: CO-FACTOR**
>
> A co-factor is a nutrient that helps *another* nutrient work better.

And don't be concerned about creating huge spikes in blood sugar; it's generally not an issue because fruits come packaged with fiber and other co-factors. However, people with diabetes or who are prone to candida or yeast infections should go easy on sugary fruits like bananas or grapes, or avoid fruits altogether until their health problem is resolved. Here are details about fruits you're likely to find on Manhattan menus:

NON-SWEET FRUITS, such as peppers, tomatoes, and cucumbers, rank low on the glycemic index and therefore barely disrupt our blood-sugar balance. People with candida or diabetes can eat them safely. During the summer, I recommend checking out the many delicious varieties of locally grown heirloom tomatoes on offer.

FATTY FRUITS, such as avocadoes and olives, are arguably the best source of fats you can eat, because they are whole and come from plants (in contrast to many processed oils). Eaten raw, as they always should be, avocadoes and olives contain a fat-digesting enzyme, lipase, that makes them easy for our bodies to process. As a bonus, they're an excellent source of protein.

BERRIES are my favorite sweet fruits, both from a culinary perspective and nutritionally speaking. On the glycemic index, they rank lowest of all the sweet fruits, and, individually, each berry is touted for a specific attribute. For instance, blueberries offer a significant number of antioxidants, while raspberries help to nourish the female reproductive system.

> **QUICK DEFINITION: GLYCEMIC INDEX**
>
> This system is a way of ranking a food's effect on your body's blood sugar level. Using the numbers one through 100, the lower the number, the lesser the impact and the lower the chance of unhealthy blood-sugar spikes.

In addition, several berries—especially goji berries and açai, the former a tart, bitter Tibetan berry, the latter the fruit of Amazonian palm trees—constitute a relatively new category of foods called superfruits, known as being exceptionally rich in nutrients. Sold in raw-food restaurants, goji berries in particular are also increasingly appearing in health-conscious eateries.

CITRUS FRUITS include oranges, lemons, limes, and grapefruits. They tend to be high in immune-boosting vitamin C and in bioflavonoids—a type of antioxidant known for its anti-cancer properties, as well as its role in keeping blood capillaries healthy. Although citrus fruits taste acidic, they are, in fact, alkalizing and help to counteract the acidity of the meat, grains and beans that typically form the bulk of a restaurant meal.

ORCHARD FRUITS include apples, pears and peaches. Best eaten raw for their enzymes, soluble fiber and nutrients, these fruits usually show up in fruit salads and smoothies.

TROPICAL FRUITS like papayas, mangoes and pineapples are especially rich in the kinds of enzymes that are not only powerful aids to digestion, but also may help to break down scar tissue and waste materials in the body. Of course, being tropical, they're not local to New

York City. Nevertheless, they offer a tasty alternative to refined sugar for someone craving a sweet snack.

Grains and Bread

In many people's minds, grains—a fresh-baked loaf of bread, pasta with tomatoes and garlic—are a bit of an indulgence, okay when eaten here or there, but not to be devoured constantly. And, actually, I agree. If you tolerate them well, grains can add fiber, protein, other nutrients and enjoyment to your diet, as long as they're properly prepared, eaten in moderation, mostly in their whole form (I'll explain shortly) and organic (many grains are heavily sprayed and genetically modified).

That's not to say there aren't drawbacks. In fact, I specifically advise my clients to avoid the complimentary bread basket served before most meals. Why? The body treats grains—especially in the form of flour—like sugar, upsetting your blood-sugar balance and contributing to weight gain and insulin resistance. In addition, unless grains are soaked or sprouted, their bran layer will contain phytic acid, which reduces mineral absorption and enzyme inhibitors, which interfere with digestion. And, overall, grains cause the body to form mucus and are acidic; this last point means that the positive, alkaline effects of eating vegetables are partially neutralized when you eat grains.

So what is the best way to eat grains? Before I answer that, I should emphasize that not all grains are created equal, whether whole or refined. To address those differences, below I discuss the pros and cons of different grains. Overall, however, I recommend eating grains in their intact state (as opposed to milled grains like flour), such as brown rice, barley, oats, quinoa and—best of all—sprouted grains, made by soaking the grain in water until it germinates. Foods that aren't intact include those made from flour like breads, cakes and pasta as well as white rice. Brown rice is whole, but pasta made from brown-rice flour isn't—although it's preferable to wheat pasta.

> **QUICK DEFINITION: REFINED GRAINS**
>
> Refined grains are made by removing the bran (the outer layer) and the germ, which is rich in vitamin E. In the removal process, the fiber and most of the nutrients are lost. This is why brown rice is preferable to white. In addition, grains are further refined when they're milled into flour for breads and pasta.

A host of reasons underpin these recommendations. Flour is prone to rancidity. It causes a big, unhealthy spike in blood sugar (because the fiber, which has been removed, isn't there to slow down the release of carbs, which upset the body's blood-sugar balance when they're released too quickly). And refined grains like white rice and bread contain plenty of calories but little nutrition.

White wheat flour is one of the worst of the refined grains. In addition to having few nutrients and containing gluten, it's usually adulterated with bleaching agents and other chemicals to enhance its performance. Unfortunately, it's used in a whopping 90 percent of baked goods. Fortunately, there are some alternatives in addition to the whole grains just discussed.

Preparation techniques make a big difference; traditional methods yield more nutritious, easier-to-digest dishes. For example, the healthiest kind of bread you can order is the aforementioned sprouted grain bread, made from presoaked grains that are baked at low temperatures. Health-food restaurants often offer them. Sourdough bread is another smart choice, since it's naturally leavened with a traditional fermentation technique that neutralizes its phytic acid, increases its nutrients' availability and creates lactobacillus—friendly gut bacteria that aid digestion. And give dosas—a fermented, regional Indian grain product—a try. Made from rice and lentils that have been fermented for at least two days, dosas have a wonderful cheesy taste. Think of them as the south Indian equivalent of burritos—but more nutritious and easier to digest. My favorite choice for breads made directly from flour is spelt and whole rye.

> **TIP: AL DENTE PASTA**
>
> Al dente is the best option for cooked pasta because it only mildly affects your blood-sugar balance; overcooked pasta causes a rapid spike in blood sugar.

Which brings me to a summary of my overall recommendations: Say yes to moderation, traditional preparation methods and whole grains—and no to refined, milled and non-organic versions. An overview of a selection of key grains follows. Although they all contain traces of gluten, I have divided them into gluten grains and non-gluten grains for people who are allergic. Even if you aren't, cutting down on gluten is good for your health.

GLUTEN GRAINS

WHEAT is the highest in gluten of all the grains, which is why it's the universal choice for bread making—gluten helps bread to rise. It's also the main ingredient in most pasta, pizza crusts, pastries, crackers, cakes, cookies and is even used as a thickener in sauces.

Given its ubiquity, wheat is not easy to avoid. That, plus the fact that it has addictive qualities, means that we tend to consume way too much of it. Nevertheless, I suggest making an effort to steer clear—or at least cut down—in part because wheat's high gluten level means it frequently disrupts the digestive system, even if you're not allergic. Reduce the percentage of wheat in your diet, and I suspect you'll be pleasantly surprised at how much better you feel day to day. (Incidentally, seitan—a popular meat substitute for vegetarians and vegans—is essentially wheat gluten with the texture of meat, so I recommend going easy on it.)

BULGUR AND COUSCOUS are actually wheat—tiny cracked pieces of it—and not a type of grain in their own right. Used like rice, bulgur is a staple in Middle Eastern restaurants and is best known as the main ingredient in tabbouleh. Couscous is typically found in North African or Moroccan cuisine.

KAMUT AND SPELT are non-hybridized, more ancient varieties of wheat. Because they're lower in gluten than wheat—and more nutritious to boot—both make good substitutes. In fact, you may do well on spelt even if you're sensitive to gluten, because the grain contains a different form of it. Fortunately, it's fairly easy to find spelt at health-conscious restaurants, where it's becoming increasingly popular as an ingredient for breads, baked goods and pizza crusts.

RYE, rich in a variety of nutrients, is used in place of wheat in items like rye bread and German pumpernickel. People who are mildly gluten sensitive tend to tolerate it in moderation. At restaurants, look for sandwiches made with whole rye.

BARLEY is one of the most ancient cultivated grains. Although it's supposed to be soothing to the intestines, it is also very acid-forming in the body.

OATS stabilize blood sugar, reduce cholesterol, and soothe the intestines and nervous system. Not usually encountered at dinner, they're most commonly served for breakfast as oatmeal or as a major component of granola and muesli. Oats also appear in some baked goods.

NON-GLUTEN GRAINS

RICE is the richest in B vitamins of all the grains and is served at all types of restaurants. It comes in numerous varieties: short-grain brown rice, which is central to the macrobiotic diet, is perhaps the most nutritious form, whereas white rice (especially the aromatic basmati) is more common than brown in Indian and Asian cuisine. Nowadays, though, most establishments offer a choice of brown or white. Brown is best; 70 percent of the nutrients and all of the fiber in white rice are lost in refining. In addition, steamed or boiled rice is preferable to fried; the latter contains damaged cooking oil.

CORN often comes from genetically modified crops, so always ask if it is organic. It turns up in restaurants as corn on the cob, as a side vegetable and in corn bread. Italian or upscale restaurants sometimes serve polenta, a mush of cornmeal usually offered as a side dish or appetizer.

BUCKWHEAT—usually in the form of the Russian staple kasha or in Japanese soba noodles—is one of a few commercial crops not routinely sprayed because it has its own natural resistance. With the longest transit time in the gut of all the grains, it is the most filling and stabilizing for blood sugar. And pre-roasting transforms buckwheat into one of the few alkalizing grains; kasha is essentially pre-roasted buckwheat.

QUINOA was a major grain for the Incas of South America. A relative newcomer to the restaurant scene, its mild taste and fluffy texture has made it enormously popular. And it's rich in high-quality protein, making it a favorite with vegetarians. If you're not familiar with quinoa, try it as an alternative to rice or oatmeal.

AMARANTH is currently not widely available in restaurants, but it is becoming increasingly popular. I recommend it to clients because it's very nutritious and contains many good amino acids such as lysine, which is low in several other grains.

MILLET, a cereal grass sometimes used in the U.S. as birdseed, but in all kinds of dishes in Asia and Africa, is another excellent option. It is alkaline, easily digested and very nutritious with a high silica content for healthy skin and bones.

Legumes

They're the punch line of bad jokes, true, but beans—as well as peas and lentils—confer many health benefits. Known as legumes, or pulses, they lower cholesterol, control blood-sugar imbalances and regulate bowel function. Low in fat (with the exception of soy beans), they're a good source of protein (especially for vegetarians and vegans), fiber and B vitamins. From a culinary perspective, herbs and spices marry well with the mild taste of legumes, which absorb the flavor of sauces and have a pleasant texture that adds bulk to any meal.

For a few susceptible individuals, abdominal gas and bloating result from eating beans, no matter how carefully they are prepared. But most of us need not avoid beans for fear of their antisocial effects. A good chef knows that most varieties of beans should be presoaked, rinsed and thoroughly cooked to break down their indigestible sugars and destroy their enzyme inhibitors (if they haven't come from a can). Here's the dish on beans:

Chickpeas, black beans, kidney beans, adzuki beans and lentils are among the legumes that crop up in numerous cultures where they have nourished humankind for millennia. For instance, chickpeas, also called garbanzo beans, are used to make the hummus and falafels of Mediterranean cuisine, as well as being popular in Indian curries; black beans are used in Mexican burritos; kidney beans are the legume of choice for chili; the adzuki bean is popular in macrobiotic restaurants; and red lentils often form the basis of dhal (dal, daal, dahl), an easily digested Indian puree.

SOY BEANS merit a lengthier discussion because they're eaten so frequently and used in so many ways—and, in particular, associated with numerous health claims and controversies.

Asians have been including soy foods in their diets for thousands of years, a fact that's often touted as the main reason for Asians' longevity and low rates of certain cancers and other Western diseases. However, this may have more to do with the paucity of dairy and meat in the Asian diet, as well as the emphasis on vegetables and various lifestyle factors. The truth is that soy has never been eaten in large quantities in Asia. Note the miso soup in Japanese restaurants, in which only a few cubes of tofu float around. And next time you order Chinese vegetables with soy-bean curd, observe how the vegetables and rice predominate. This marginal role for soy stands in stark contrast to the modern soy burger at the center of the vegetarian entrée.

Over the past few decades, vegetarians and vegans in particular have become overreliant on soy because it is a balanced protein and can be formed into mock meat. Restaurants dutifully offer soy, often in the form of tofu, as the vegetarian option for protein.

However, studies detailing soy's high nutrient content and positive effects have recently been contested by additional research. Soy is known to block the absorption of some nutrients and is thought to increase the likelihood of ovarian and breast cancer. For more information, check out *The Whole Soy Story: The Dark Side of America's Favorite Health Food* by Dr. Kaayla Daniel; the book investigates the health problems linked to the overconsumption of soy.

One solution is simply to cut back. Another is to be mindful of the kinds of soy products you consume. Organic, non-GMO soy is your best bet, as are soy products like miso, soy yogurt, natto and tempeh, all of which undergo a fermentation process in which otherwise non-viable nutrients are partly predigested—and phytates and enzyme inhibitors that cause gastric distress are neutralized. In addition, those forms of soy are endowed with probiotics. With the possible exception of soy yogurt, these healthy forms of soy are usually available in Chinese, Japanese and macrobiotic restaurants.

Tofu, perhaps the most ubiquitous form of soy in restaurants, provides some nutrition but should be eaten in moderation since it hasn't undergone the all-important fermentation process. As for edamame, it's a whole food but not easy to digest—good for you, but not in excess, that is.

Soy milk, soy ice cream and soy cheese, however, are highly processed and not fermented—best consumed only on occasion. They usually come with additives of one kind or another, in an attempt to mimic the flavor and texture of the real thing.

Desserts made from hemp, almonds or rice are better choices. There's even an amazing raw, vegan ice cream made from cashews and sweetened with agave in New York State, available at organicnectars. com; persuade your neighborhood chef to place an order. Raw-food restaurants are likely to place this ice cream—or perhaps the chef's own creation—on the dessert menu.

A soy product that should be completely avoided whenever possible is textured vegetable (or soy) protein, also known as TVP, which in similar forms goes by the names protein soy isolate or hydrolyzed plant (or soy) protein. Made from soybean meal after the oil has been processed out with chemicals and intense pressure, TVP is used in veggie burgers and fake meats. TVP, soy isolate and hydrolyzed soy bear a close chemical resemblance to plastic and may contain residues from processing, including petroleum solvents, sulphuric acids, hydrochloric acid and caustic soda. Those are just a few good reasons to bypass that fake turkey sandwich in favor of the Tempeh Reuben.

MEAT STILL ENJOYS A reputation as being as all-American as the Wild West and cowboy boots. But improving yourself is an all-American quality, too, and to do that it's best to cut down on your intake of animal products, including fish, meat, poultry, dairy and eggs. I'm not saying that you have to become vegetarian or vegan, though; each individual should do what's best for his or her body.

THE FOURTH PRECEPT: If you choose to eat animal products, consume only (a) high-quality and sustainably raised animals (ideally pasture-raised and grass-fed, but at least hormone and antibiotic-free); and do so (b) in moderation—meaning smaller portions with less frequency.

Remember how proponents of The China Study argue that meat-eating is a leading cause of human disease, but followers of the nutritionist Weston A. Price say that it can be beneficial? That's not the only area of contention regarding animal products. Another is over whether animal fats cause heart disease. An increasingly vocal minority of researchers claim that the cholesterol myth is just that—a myth. They believe that highly processed vegetable oils and hydrogenated fats are more artery-clogging and lead to more heart trouble than lard. Of course, adherents of veganism and vegetarianism eschew animal products for a variety of reasons, while others believe that those diets are lacking in some essential nutrients such as vitamins B12 and D.

Different people will side with different research; your genetic makeup or lifestyle may mean that eating meat is necessary for your body to function smoothly. To figure it out, I advocate experimenting and also thinking about how certain foods and dietary principles make you feel.

If you consume animal products, I hope that you do so in moderation. Why? Well, for one thing, eating too many provides more protein than necessary for human health, creating more acidity than the body can process and leading to problems like fatigue and osteoporosis. In addition, there's substantial evidence that the practice of raising animals for human consumption—especially in conventional corporate feedlots—is unsustainable and environmentally problematic. Easy ways to lower the percentage of animal products in your diet include thinking of meat as a side dish rather than a main course, as well as eating smaller portions less frequently.

In addition, make sure that all of the animal products you consume—beef, dairy, eggs, chicken and so on—come from high-quality, organic and pasture-fed animals. As well as having no fiber, animal products are a concentrated source of the medications, stress, hormones and environmental toxins that the animal has been exposed to. That's a powerful argument for choosing an organic, pasture-fed animal, which won't have been subjected to stressful conditions or injected with toxins like hormones and antibiotics. Instead, it will have been raised similarly to the way it would have been in the wild: a pasture-raised cow, for instance, grazes on grass, gets exercise and is exposed to the sun, all of which results in a healthy cow—and extra benefits for us.

> **REMINDER: DON'T NECESSARILY WORRY ABOUT ORGANIC CERTIFICATION**
>
> Small farmers who raise animals sustainably and hormone- and antibiotic-free often can't afford to obtain the accreditation "certified organic."

To summarize: make sure that the animal products you eat are high quality and organic (that is, hormone- and antibiotic-free) and preferably grass-fed. In addition, consume them less often and in small portions—and eat them with vegetables (especially leafy greens) to counteract some of the potential negative effects. By making those tweaks, you ensure that high-quality meat, fish, poultry, dairy and eggs can become a healthy part of a balanced diet rather than a risk factor. In the following two sections, I round up the different kinds of animal foods appearing on restaurant menus.

Meat and Fish

Not all meats are created equal. Some are organic, some not; some grilled, others fried. Part of the purpose of this section is to further clarify and help you choose the healthiest options.

For instance, grilled or roasted meats are better for you than deep-fried dishes. Be aware, though, that meats smoked or barbecued on charcoal grills can develop a carcinogen called polycyclic aromatic hydrocarbons. Like most other foods, meat is best for your body when it has been cooked briefly and gently. Prolonged high heat reduces the amount of vitamins and minerals in meat and denatures its protein. Worse, it increases the toxicity of contaminants already there, such as nitrates and pesticides. Of course, with the disease-causing pathogens showing up in animal products, it may not be such a bad idea to avoid rare or raw meat (which otherwise would be the healthiest way to consume high-quality, properly raised animal products). However, when possible, ask that your meat not be overcooked. Medium-rare is a good option and usually what chefs prefer anyway.

Some foods digest well when eaten with specific kinds of dishes, while other foods are the opposite—concentrated starches and concentrated proteins, for instance, should be eaten separately. The idea behind food-combining is to eat the former category of foods together, and to separate the latter. Protein causes the body to produce specific enzymes and hydrochloric acid, which increases the stomach's acidity; starches need an alkaline environment for digestion. Translation: Eating a lot of meat with starches like bread or potatoes can cause gas and indigestion. A food-combining solution: Pair heavy proteins like meat with vegetables, such as leafy greens, instead of with starches like breads, grains and potatoes.

Here are details about the different types of meats you're likely to encounter on menus:

BEEF is a source of iron and vitamin B12, as well as essential fats. Cows raised in pastures—where they're exposed to the sun and eat grass—provide the healthiest meat; in fact, an essential fat and anti-cancer nutrient called conjugated linoleic acid (CLA) occurs only in grass-fed animals.

One rung down from grass-fed cows is organic beef, which means that the animal has been raised without hormones and antibiotics, but has been fed grains, corn or organic vegetarian feed. Often this is for taste reasons but sometimes even these animals are overfed in an attempt to fatten them up, a practice that makes them more prone to disease. Since grass is the natural diet for cows, animals that eat grains or corn—even if it's high-quality organic—are not as healthy as their grass-fed counterparts and therefore not as healthy for humans.

And as far as factory-farmed beef goes, I advise avoiding it altogether because of the health, environmental and moral issues involved. Jammed together in pens where they never see sunlight and are injected with hormones and who knows what else, the cows raised in such farms are usually very sick—part of the reason they're injected with excess antibiotics. That's an excellent reason to opt for grass-fed, sustainably raised beef—or, at the very least, a hormone and antibiotic-free animal.

While better quality meats may be a tad pricey, think of this as a motivator for you to eat less meat overall; as you may recall, I'm a big proponent of eating meat in moderation.

CHICKEN, LAMB and **PORK**, all sources of protein, can be good for you, like beef, if you choose an organic, naturally raised animal and eat it in moderation.

When it comes to pork, though, don't be fooled by the advertising ("The New White Meat"). It's actually probably less healthy for you than chicken or lamb. And it makes such a difference to your health that I'll say it again: order free-range, naturally fed chicken, lamb or pork—and consume small portions.

GAME ANIMALS like bison and venison are among the healthiest kinds of meats because they come from freshly killed animals that lived in the wild. These animals are leaner than beef or chicken and boast a higher proportion of omega-3 fatty acids. In addition, they're less likely to be contaminated or diseased. It is becoming easier to find bison and venison in trendy restaurants, as well as establishments emphasizing organic dishes, although, for some, venison's gamey flavor is an acquired taste.

CURED MEATS like sausages, luncheon meats and bacon can be okay to eat in moderation; it all comes down to how they are raised and made. I recommend cutting out luncheon meats altogether—nearly all of them contain carcinogenic preservatives such as nitrates. If you can't stay away from, say, bologna, at least get a package labeled "nitrate-free." Two requirements should be met before you purchase bacon or sausage: (1) The meat should have come from a good-quality animal, one that was naturally raised and fed (hormone- and antibiotic-free). (2) The way the meat was made should be as natural as possible. Sausage without casings or fillers, produced on the premises at an organic restaurant, for instance, gets my thumbs-up—as long as you eat it in moderation.

FOIE GRAS and **VEAL** tend to be served only in upscale restaurants; the former is the liver of a fattened-up goose or duck, and the latter is the meat of a milk-fed (or sometimes formula-fed) baby calf.

A lot of people avoid veal and foie gras (French for "fat liver") for moral reasons. Since I don't see any particular health benefits from eating either of these foods, I recommend avoiding them altogether.

COLD-WATER FISH like salmon, mackerel, cod and sardines, are chock-full of heart-healthy omega 3 fatty acids as well as fat-soluble vitamins and minerals, including iodine. Unfortunately, these goodies are meaningless if the fish is conventionally farm-raised, a technique that results in more PCBs, mercury and disease—and fewer omega 3's. Plus, the feed for farmed salmon usually contains dye to give the flesh a pink color.

If you want the benefits of organically farm-raised or wild fish, salmon—a potent source of omega 3—is probably the easiest fish to find at restaurants. Most nutritious in its raw form (for instance, as sushi), it's also healthy when steamed or baked. Skip tempura, though; it involves dipping fish in batter before deep-frying it in hot oil.

SCAVENGER FISH include tuna, swordfish, carp and catfish. They eat almost anything they find in the sea, including already-dead fish (yum!). That's why their tissues are likely to contain the toxins of other fish, like PCBs and mercury; it's also why scavenger fish are considered no-no's for women who are pregnant or breastfeeding. If you like fish, I suggest sticking mostly to the cold-water kind.

SHELLFISH is a category that includes scallops, clams, mussels, oysters, shrimp, crabs and lobsters. They should be eaten in moderation and always while very fresh and in season. For a number of reasons, I am not a huge fan. Shellfish spoil easily and are a common cause of food

> **INTERESTING TIDBIT: ORGAN MEATS**
>
> A few nutritionally-minded types, including followers of Weston A. Price, believe that the healthiest part of an animal to eat is its organs, like the liver—as long as it comes from a properly-raised animal (when we consume meat, we tend to eat steak, which is a muscle).

poisoning, as well as being prone to contamination. Be sure yours are sourced from clean waters.

To help you make quality seafood choices when you're shopping or out to eat, download the *Seafood Pocket Guide* at (http://edf.org/documents/1980_pocket_seafood_selector.pdf). It lists fish both high in omega-3 fats and low in environmental contaminants.

Dairy and Eggs

Cheese conjures up sophisticated images like wine-and-cheese parties, while milk perhaps sounds quaint (think milkmen in the 1950s). Like those varying images, dairy and eggs have varying effects on your health, depending on who you are, how much you eat and the quality of what you consume. Frankly, I'm not the biggest advocate of consuming a lot of dairy, but I try to stay open-minded.

Dairy's big selling point is that it's a source of calcium. Yet milk's acidity means that it actually leaches calcium from the bones. In addition, its low magnesium content in relation to its calcium (they are required in balance for proper utilization) means that the calcium may not get completely used by the body. It's better obtained from vegetables, seeds and nuts.

Another reason I'm not a big fan of dairy products is their tendency to create mucus in the body, resulting in anything from a runny nose to a clogged-up digestive system.

In addition, many people are lactose intolerant; only around a third of the world's population possesses the genetic mutation required for the proper digestion of dairy. Asian and African-American populations include an especially high percentage of milk-intolerant individuals, which is why you're not likely to find many dairy products on the menu at an Asian restaurant.

That doesn't mean dairy is the devil, at least not for people who digest it well—as long as you get it from grass-fed cows, or at minimum, opt for an organic version. I recommend avoiding products containing Recombinant Bovine Growth Hormone, aka RBGH, a genetically engineered drug associated with growth abnormalities and malignant tumors. Another reason to go organic: dairy cows fed unnatural diets, forced to produce excessive quantities of milk, confined to small stalls or kept in unhygienic conditions often suffer from infected udders. This infection, called mastitis, causes the sick cows to release pus into their milk.

A roundup of dairy products commonly found in restaurants follows.

MILK itself doesn't feature prominently on most menus, but it crops up in sauces, smoothies and as a side dish for tea and coffee. Too much cow's milk will provide more protein than we need and can cause weight gain. Some organic-focused restaurants offer preferable alternatives like rice, almond or hemp milk (note that I didn't include soy, which I addressed earlier); ask the staff if you don't see any of those options on the menu.

CHEESE is often a concentrated form of milk, best eaten in moderation. Some of my clients who want to reduce their cheese consumption find it extremely hard to do so; cheese is considered one of the most difficult foods to stop eating (in addition to sugar) because of its casein, a protein with addictive qualities.

One partial solution is to eat better types of cheese, like raw (unpasteurized) versions, which retain more enzymes and nutrients, and boast an arguably better taste than their pasteurized counterparts. Although they're not yet common in the United States, with demand, their availability is increasing, particularly in restaurants that stress organic or specialty foods.

Sheep and goat cheeses are another smart alternative. Easier to digest than cheese made from cow's milk, these cheeses are increasingly popular in restaurants, where you might find them atop salads and as sandwich fillings.

And no surprise here: I recommend avoiding processed cheese, a staple in some sandwiches and fast-food entrées; they usually contain additives such as emulsifiers, extenders, phosphates and hydrogenated oils. You'll likely find them easy to give up, considering their bland taste and plastic texture.

CULTURED DAIRY PRODUCTS—kefir, yogurt and sour cream—are easier to digest than other dairy items because their lactose and casein are already partially broken down. Kefir is a liquid yogurt traditionally created from camel's milk, although many versions use cow's milk. Most Greek and Indian restaurants serve yogurt; the latter may also use ghee in food preparation. Well tolerated by most people, ghee is butter with the milk solids removed.

BUTTER most often appears at your table accompanying a complimentary basket of bread. Unless you have a dairy allergy, a moderate amount of butter—especially organic—offers some benefits, including easily digested fats and the fat-soluble vitamins A and D.

ICE CREAM and **CREAM** populate the dessert section of many menus. Practice moderation, or try some of the naturally sweetened nut-based ice creams popping up at raw-food restaurants.

EGGS are often classified with dairy products (especially by vegetarians) because, like milk and cheese, they come from animals but the animals don't have to be killed to obtain the food. Rich in vitamins, minerals and protein, eggs can be quite nourishing.

> **TIP:**
> **EAT THE WHOLE EGG**
>
> The yolk contains a good deal of nutrients the whites just don't provide like anti-inflammatory choline and antioxidant lutein. Plus, the yolk promotes a healthy HDL/LDL cholesterol ratio. So eat the whole shebang, yolk and whites. Your body will thank you.

Their cholesterol content causes debate, however; overcooked, it becomes oxidized, meaning it transforms from a useful nutrient into a potentially harmful chemical. For that reason (i.e., they contain oxidized cholesterol), avoid powdered eggs, which have been through a heating and drying process. To avoid oxidation in your egg order, ask for lightly poached or sunny-side-up eggs rather than scrambled or fried; similarly, soft-boiled trumps hard-boiled. Raw eggs are even more beneficial than the lightly cooked kind. However, people susceptible to salmonella, such as the elderly, the infirm or pregnant women, should avoid raw eggs.

As with dairy and meat, a chef's choice of egg supplier has implications for both nutritional quality and taste. Battery-caged hens tend to turn out eggs with salmonella, few nutrients and a bland or fishy taste—and the cruelty of crowding hens together is another reason to skip ordering such eggs. Free-range, pasture-raised hens, on the other hand, produce unpredictable eggs; as with heirloom vegetables, the result is a richer flavor and increased nutrient content. At the very least, stick with hormone- and antibiotic-free eggs taken from cage-free hens.

IN THE NEXT SECTION, I discuss the kinds of things that make your mouth water—sweeteners, seasonings, fats and oils, and beverages. These more subtle foods may be potentially harmful, but they don't have to be, as long as you approach these full-of-flavor foods the right way. Which brings me to my final premise, one that by now you know, but which I'd like to highlight once more.

THE FIFTH PRECEPT: To feel better immediately, simply reduce your intake of artificial, chemical-laden processed foods as well as sugar, caffeine and alcohol.

As you read through the next few categories, keep this precept in mind. It's actually less difficult to follow than you might think; stick to the natural flavorings, not the substances created in a test tube. Do those long, chemical, hard-to-pronounce names even sound that tasty? Not really, right? Educating yourself about all of the tasty *and* natural substances out there (honey, anyone?) is the perfect insurance against being lured away by processed foods.

Fats and Oils

They've got a less-than-savory rep, but don't be afraid of fats and oils. They play an important role in the human diet.

Fats and oils slow the release of sugar from other foods, create a feeling of satisfaction, give us a source of energy and allow us to absorb fat-soluble vitamins, including A, D, E and K by carrying them across the gut wall. In addition, our bodies use fats as building materials, incorporating them into the cell membranes to create the right balance between firmness and flexibility.

We like to preach about its evils—weight gain, heart disease—while still associating fatty food with comfort and fun. Truth is, it can get kind of complicated, so let's simplify. The list of different fats and oils is a long one, so here's what you need to know about the ones you are most likely to encounter at a restaurant.

Trans fats or hydrogenated oils, made by injecting hydrogen into liquid vegetable oils to make them more solid, should be completely avoided as they are probably the most harmful ingredient in our food supply. In fact, New York City has ensured you'll avoid these oils because in 2008, the city banned the use of trans fats in restaurants. So it is far less likely than before that dining out will mean consuming damaged vegetable oils in the form of vegetable shortening and hydrogenated margarine.

Avocadoes, raw nuts and seeds, coconuts and olives should form the bulk of your fat intake and are excellent sources of essential fatty acids, fiber and other co-factors (when these foods are turned into oils, some of these goodies are eliminated). These plant fats should not cause weight gain as part of a balanced diet, nor should they contribute to heart disease.

Whole coconut meat is preferable to coconut oil or coconut butter, although those latter two don't deserve the artery-blocking image painted by some, even though they are a saturated fat. Want to learn more? Take a look at *The Healing Properties of Coconut Oil* by nutritionist Bruce Fife.

HEMP SEEDS and FLAXSEEDS are valued for their essential fatty acids, but they are best used whole and raw since processing, storage and heating can turn these delicate oils rancid. Flax, like fish, contains high levels of omega 3 (minus contaminants such as mercury and PCBs), but you can't cook with flax oil—it's best to eat the seeds. Hemp and flax oils are healthy only when cold-pressed; in that form, they make an excellent salad dressing.

OLIVE OIL is a monounsaturated fat. Even though it has negligible amounts of essential fatty acids, it's better than many other oils and doesn't contain a high amount of harmful omega 6. And the form in which it's served at most quality restaurants—as salad dressing—is good, since it has more benefits when raw, especially if it's extra virgin, organic and cold-pressed. It crops up in that form at Italian and Mediterranean establishments. Like most oils, though, olive oil is damaged by high heat.

BUTTER has become cool again after the downfall of margarine because of its dangerous levels of trans fat (hydrogenated oils). I believe butter—especially organic butter from a grass-fed cow—has some health benefits when consumed in moderation. Margarine, on the other hand, can damage your arteries more than any amount of butterfat because of its aforementioned trans fats. Its overuse in recent years—along with oils like soy, sunflower and corn—has contributed to a national over-consumption of omega 6 fats versus omega 3, a situation that has been linked to numerous health problems.

Salt and Seasonings

My friends like to tease that I have a "salt tooth" in contrast to most people's "sweet tooth," but I've learned to treat salt as I would sugar—with fondness but also caution.

Salt provides sodium, an important mineral involved in many bodily processes. However, it's unhealthy when you're getting a lot of sodium but hardly any potassium, a mineral found mainly in fresh fruits and vegetables. That's because sodium and potassium work together as intimate partners. It is essential that they remain in proper balance for the smooth functioning of our muscles, lungs, heart and nervous system, as well as for the water balance within our bodies. In particular, many people suffer from raised blood pressure, muscle cramps and water retention when they consume too much salt.

Most people get *way* more than enough salt whether they try to or not, just because salt, and therefore sodium, is overabundant in our modern, processed meals. Potassium, however, is lacking, because we don't eat enough vegetables. We need less than half a teaspoon of sodium per day, but many of us are consuming *seven* times that amount.

At a restaurant, you can request that your meal be prepared with less salt. You'll be amazed at how quickly you lose the desire for excess salt and start to find too much unappealing—I certainly have, despite my "salt tooth."

TIP: GOOD SALT SUBSTITUTES

One clever and healthful way to reduce your sodium intake at a restaurant is to ask for extra garlic, ginger, herbs or spices to be substituted instead, a move that will increase the flavor of your meal while adding some health benefits. Some of the best additions are garlic, a natural antibiotic; ginger, an anti-inflammatory and digestive aid; cayenne, a circulation enhancer; turmeric, an antioxidant and anti-inflammatory; and green herbs such as parsley or cilantro, a good source of vitamins and chlorophyll.

REFINED TABLE SALT tends to be processed and altered with chemicals—it's sodium chloride with no nutritional benefits. I recommend deleting it from your diet, since it contributes to the sodium-potassium imbalance described above and usually contains aluminum to boot.

KOSHER SALT is a coarse salt with no additives; its thick crystal grains help to cure meat, thus its name (since it's used by some Jews to make meat kosher). Foodies like this salt for its texture and taste; perhaps because it appears in gourmet foods, it's sometimes thought to be healthier than table salt. That's not the case, however; there's no nutritional difference between table and kosher salt (the latter may be marginally more healthful because it doesn't have additives, but don't be fooled into thinking it's good for you).

SEA SALT or **HIMALAYAN CRYSTAL SALT** both appear at some restaurants and are fine to eat in moderation. Natural and unprocessed, they contain minerals from the ocean, have a better flavor than table salt and tend to be prized by top chefs. Although sea and crystal salt are gaining in popularity, they're still currently most likely to crop up in the kitchens of health-food or gourmet restaurants. At raw-food restaurants, they're usually the only kind of salt offered.

BRAGG'S LIQUID AMINOS is a low-sodium alternative to soy sauce (although it's made from soy beans) that appears on the tables of many health-food restaurants. Although it's better than table salt, I tend not to think of it as a health food. Despite its name, the amount of amino acids (i.e., protein) that it provides is negligible. And like soy sauce, it has been found to contain some naturally occurring monosodium glutamate (MSG), a flavor-enhancer that has been associated with various health problems. Nevertheless, it does add a strong, savory flavor to meals.

SHOYU and **TAMARI**, both commonly referred to as soy sauce, are more or less interchangeable; both are fermented soy condiments, except that tamari is wheat-free. Asian and health-food restaurants serve shoyu and tamari, where they're sometimes also used for stir-frying. Health conscious diners prefer naturally brewed versions over highly processed and additive-laden cheaper imitations. However, I find soy sauce a questionable substitute for table salt because of the soy, wheat and the inevitable processing. Unless stated on the label, soy sauce is not a low-sodium alternative and is best used sparingly.

Sweeteners

"You're sweet." "How sweet it is." "That's *sweet*." The English language is peppered with instances of how, well, *sweet* sweetness is. So it's understandable that sugary foods are where I get the most resistance and guilt from my clients.

It's not exactly a news flash that refined white sugar and the more insidious high fructose corn syrup is bad for us. It's difficult to get away from, though, because sugar is in all kinds of foods—not just bottled drinks and desserts, but also savory sauces.

Even if we're aware of which foods contain refined white sugar, it's hard not to order them anyway. That's because sugar is addictive. Stop eating it and you'll experience withdrawal symptoms. Eat some and you will crave more. Sounds like an addiction to me. Then there's the emotional aspect of sugar cravings. Consider how children are offered sweets if they're "good" or "behave." To make matters worse, it seems that we have been biologically programmed to seek out sweetness as a way to avoid poison, which tends to be bitter. But I bet evolution intended for us to eat fruits and not, say, doughnuts.

Even though you know that sweets aren't good for you, it's worth pointing out the many ways they're bad. Sugar is an anti-nutrient, not only giving the body zero nutrition, but actually robbing us of goodies. Plus, it's probably the major contributor to weight gain; at a certain point of saturation, the body converts it to fat, putting excess sugar into storage in order to quickly remove it from the blood where it would otherwise create havoc. After all, there is only so much sugar that we can use as energy. Sugar has been linked to a variety of other ailments, from lowered immunity and poor gut flora to cancer and diabetes.

Yet, according to the USDA, we are eating increasingly more sugar. The average American consumes over a cup a day of the stuff—an increase of 23 percent between 1985 and 1999.

So what should we do? Well, we have to be really smart about our approach. Something I have noticed with my clients is that once they begin to take better care of themselves in other areas of their lives and eat better-quality foods, their cravings tend to lessen. Sometimes exercise helps, as does eating a little more protein and drinking more water. I always suggest a switch to more natural, gentler forms of sweeteners. Take these steps and over time you will gradually experience refined sugar as being too sweet and tasting fake. True, it may take a while, but I've found that this approach has worked, not only for me but for many former sugar addicts with whom I've worked.

Let's take a look at some of the common sweeteners you will encounter at restaurants.

WHITE TABLE SUGAR, HIGH FRUCTOSE CORN SYRUP and even **BROWN SUGAR** should be avoided as much as possible.

ORGANIC RAW CANE SUGAR, FLORIDA CRYSTALS and **TURBINADO SUGAR** have gained in popularity and are commonly found on the tables and in desserts at health-food restaurants. Although I am not a big fan and don't use them myself, I believe they are a slightly better option than the completely refined stuff, since these kinds of sugars do retain some nutrients and are better for the environment. But they're not healthy.

MAPLE SYRUP and **BROWN RICE SYRUP** are preferable to all of the above. They are the most commonly consumed natural sweeteners. While not ideal because they can negatively impact existing digestive issues and have a fairly high glycemic index, they are okay in moderation if they are pure and of a high quality.

HONEY is a far better choice than many of the other sweeteners, especially the raw, unheated varieties, which are rich in antioxidants, enzymes and various healing co-factors.

RAW AGAVE NECTAR has fast become the sweetener of choice among those looking to avoid refined sugar. I believe it's a better option than refined sugar, yet it still has its issues, including a very high fructose content and production quality. I suggest using it in moderation.

STEVIA (technically a supplement), extracted from the sweet leaves of the stevia plant, is also becoming increasingly popular for its highly sugary taste and safeness for diabetics, although some people are not crazy about its aftertaste. In addition, although it has been used safely by humans for a long time, there is conflicting research in regard to its safety.

More and more restaurants are providing agave and stevia for tea or coffee, as well as using them in place of sugar in desserts and baked goods.

ARTIFICIAL SWEETENERS like Splenda, Equal or NutraSweet (aspartame) should be avoided. There are more adverse reactions to NutraSweet reported to the FDA than to all other foods and additives combined. Plus, there is even convincing evidence that these artificial sweeteners lead to weight gain.

Beverages

A sparkling stream of water runs through a picturesque valley. This could be an ad for anything from beer to an energy drink. The point? Advertisers know that we know that water is good for us. So they use it to sell beverages that aren't so good. Read on for details about the drinks you'll find at restaurants.

WATER should be your beverage of choice, in my opinion; usually it's the most natural and purest liquid you can get. Bottled water in restaurants tends to be overpriced, but it may be worth it if the only other option is unfiltered tap water, which will be polluted by chlorine and fluoride, among other contaminants. Filtered tap water is the best option; it's free, safe and better for the environment than bottled water (plus, you avoid ingesting chemicals that may leach into the water from the plastic bottle). If the restaurant's water is filtered, the food that's cooked in it will be safer for you as well.

> **TIP: WATER TEMPERATURE**
>
> Room-temperature water is the healthiest kind. That's because ice-cold water is difficult to digest, so ask for yours with no ice—but with a slice of lemon, which makes the water more alkalizing and cleansing.

FRUIT JUICES are okay to drink but quite sugary, which is why I recommend diluting them with water. **VEGETABLE JUICES**: much better. They count toward your nutrient intake, especially with dark greens thrown in.

SODAS and **SOFT DRINKS** are composed of unfiltered, artificially carbonated water with added sugar (or, worse, corn syrup or artificial sweeteners), flavorings, colorings, preservatives and sometimes caffeine. In addition, their high phosphoric-acid content is associated with osteoporosis. Not a recipe for health. I recommend avoiding them altogether, especially the diet ones, which are loaded with artificial sweeteners that, research has suggested, actually may cause weight gain.

As long as they're sweetened with fruit juice instead of cane sugar, natural sodas are fine to drink in moderation, since they're made from cleaner water and are caffeine-free.

COFFEE, provided by most restaurants, can provide a much-needed lift. Still, my recommendation is to reduce caffeine consumption with the goal of eventually giving it up altogether. Sure, coffee beans may contain antioxidants; plus, some people metabolize caffeine better than others. However, caffeine in general, and coffee in particular, is linked to raised blood pressure, insomnia, nervous conditions, osteoporosis and certain cancers. At the very least, imbibing caffeine with your meal reduces the availability of minerals in the food—it leaches them out.

If you can't resist ordering a cup, check whether the restaurant offers an organic, fair-trade or shade-grown version.

GREEN TEA may be the most healthful, or at least the most benign, of all caffeinated beverages. That's because it contains polyphenols, a type of antioxidant that can reduce blood pressure (note coffee's opposite effect), lower blood fats and combat those free radicals we encounter in a city environment. It contains much less caffeine than coffee. In addition, it has theanine, which mitigates some of caffeine's effects to produce a calmer type of energy and prevents a caffeine "hangover."

TIP: COFFEE REPLACEMENT

• Raw cacao beans, or nibs, make a tasty interim crutch for people trying to break their coffee habit. Cacao will give you a lift—partially from caffeine, and partially from other natural happiness-inducing chemicals. Plus, it's extraordinarily rich in magnesium and antioxidants (sorry, chocolate bars with their cooked cacao and sugar don't count as a whole-food alternative to coffee). Restaurants that serve raw or live desserts—meaning enzymes and healthy bacteria are active in the food—often offer a raw cacao fix, sweetened with agave nectar to boot.
• Green tea, which contains less caffeine than coffee and has energy-giving theanine, offers a healthful boost.
• Grain coffee substitutes, especially popular in macrobiotic restaurants, are caffeine-free yet have coffee's robust taste.

BLACK TEA has fewer antioxidants and more caffeine than green. But it doesn't contain as much caffeine as coffee, unless it is steeped for an especially long time.

Both green and black tea come from the same plant, often one that's been heavily sprayed, so seek out an organic version.

DECAFFEINATED TEA or **COFFEE** is fine to drink if the caffeine has been removed using the Swiss-water process. Otherwise, residue from chemicals used to remove the caffeine might remain—a non-issue if the product is certified organic. And note that all decaffeinated beverages still contain some traces of caffeine.

HERBAL TEAS may be the best hot drink overall, since they are naturally caffeine-free and boast mild therapeutic benefits. For instance, peppermint and ginger tea both are helpful to drink after a heavy meal, since they aid digestion; chamomile, as you probably know, has calming properties.

FERMENTED DRINKS are digestive aids, rich in enzymes and probiotics. They tend to be offered by establishments that focus on traditional health foods. Kombucha tea is not technically a tea, but rather a fermented cold drink made by steeping a mushroomlike growth in water. Rich in enzymes, probiotics and B vitamins, kombucha is a wonderful aid to digestion and general well-being. A "live" product, this tea is popular in raw- and health-food restaurants. Other common kinds of fermented drinks include amazake, made from rice; kefir, which is lacto-fermented milk; and ginger ale and apple cider, both healthy when made using old-fashioned methods.

WINE is fermented, true, but I believe that its alcohol content tends to neutralize the much-touted health benefits. Although wine has been in the news as being good for you in various small ways, my experience is that people use that as an excuse to drink too much. Even in relatively small amounts, wine is an anti-nutrient, particularly good at robbing the body of B vitamins. All alcohol can make you accident prone, dehydrated, unable to concentrate and even aggressive. It should be avoided if you are susceptible to candida overgrowth. And it's worth repeating: long-term drinking to excess, whether labeled alcoholism or not, can result in liver damage and stomach ulcers, not to mention a host of social and emotional problems.

Still, like coffee, alcohol can be useful in moderation. After a stressful day at work, a relaxing glass of wine can make all the difference to your enjoyment of a meal and your ability to converse with fellow diners. Plus, it can stimulate the digestive process. Red wine in particular provides some antioxidant benefits and is said to be good for the heart in moderate amounts. As with coffee, though, there is no need to rely on wine for your antioxidants; think vegetables and fruits instead.

If you do choose to consume alcohol, organic beer or red wine is the best choice; like other organic goods, these drinks should be free of pesticides. And biodynamic wine is arguably better than regular organic, since biodynamic producers go to extraordinary lengths to create special, pure growing conditions.

Restaurants with an extensive wine list may offer one labeled sulphite-free or NSA, meaning "no sulphites added." Sulphites occur naturally on grapes, but many vineyards add more to prevent bacterial growth, oxidation and a vinegary taste. Many people experience allergic side effects, including headaches, when they consume sulphites, and some connoisseurs prefer the taste of a low-sulphite wine. White wine generally has fewer sulphites than red.

BEER, ALE and **LAGER** are lower in alcohol than wine, but it's still important to watch the amount that you drink.

HARD LIQUOR or **SPIRITS** such as vodka, tequila, or rum are much higher in alcohol than both wine and beer, which is why they're often diluted with tonic water or fruit juice. Be especially careful of these because of the high alcohol content.

MAKING IT ALL WORK

I'M NOT THE KIND of guy to just hand you the facts and run. What do you do now that I've provided an education about different foods? Well, first let's remind ourselves what those *Five Precepts* are:

1 There's more than one right way to eat.
2 The overwhelming majority of your diet should consist of natural, high-quality and whole foods.
3 Everyone would be better off if a larger proportion of their diet consisted of plants—mostly vegetables (in particular, leafy greens), and some nuts, seeds and fruits.
4 If you choose to eat animal products, consume only (a) high-quality and sustainably raised animals (ideally pasture-raised and grass-fed, but at least hormone and antibiotic-free); and do so (b) in moderation—meaning smaller portions with less frequency.
5 To feel better immediately, simply reduce your intake of artificial, chemical-laden processed foods as well as sugar, caffeine and alcohol.

I want to make it easy for you to transition—and stick—to healthier dining, so here are several psychological and social tips for following the precepts outlined above.

The Right Approach
MOTIVATION
This is the *why*: You've got to know why you're doing something to be able to really carry it out.

So, why are you changing your diet? Okay, I confess. We all, including me, want to be slimmer, trimmer, better looking. And those are okay reasons. But there are better reasons, like heightened energy, greater strength, fewer illnesses and clearer thinking. I find that it helps to get excited about getting the most out of life and bringing enjoyment not only to yourself, but also to other people—not to mention planet earth— since our food choices have a major impact on the environment.

So, right now, take out a sheet of paper and write down *why* you want to eat healthier. Once you've written down your motivations, commit to them—that is, setting a clear intention. It's a great launching pad for getting—and staying—motivated.

The other part of intention and motivation? Believing that, yes, you can do this. Don't simply hope you can succeed; know that you will.

AWARENESS
Awareness means (a) remembering your motivation (your *why*) and intention (your commitment); and (b) being aware of the various forces that might act against you. Admitting that challenges exist is a necessary step to moving beyond them.

These challenges include: physical cravings and addictions, emotional attachments to food, cultural conditioning, advertising and a lack of education about healthy eating. Peer pressure is another biggie; you're going to need to keep your resolve if others try to coax you back to your old ways. Just be aware that change can make others uncomfortable.

Realize that these scenarios are not personal to you. They are issues for all of us, since we are all human and ever-evolving. Therefore, be aware that you are not a victim.

Awareness also means paying attention to how certain foods make us feel, physically and mentally. Keep a diet diary if that helps. Begin to eliminate any foods or drinks that drain your energy, give you indigestion, make you irritable or create so much guilt when you consume them that you simply don't enjoy or digest them properly.

PATIENCE

Do you wish I had a magic formula for positive change? Actually, I do. Think of it as the magical trio: patience, perseverance and resilience. Okay, I admit it: those qualities aren't so simple.

In dietary terms, those words mean realizing that lasting improvements take time and application. At first you may need to be satisfied with eating healthier about half of the time, but once you do get to that 50/50 mark, you will have the momentum to go further, slowly, going from 60/40 to 70/30 and onward, until you may even hit 90/10. Don't be too extreme right away, though. Just start with the 50 percent rule and see what happens. En route, don't be discouraged by slip-ups. Just notice it and move on.

> **YOUR CHOICES AS AN INDIVIDUAL**
>
> Part of being human is having the ability to make conscious choices based on our intentions and what is best for us.

After a while, you'll notice that, bit by bit, you're starting to find excess sugar and salt unpalatable. In the meantime, instead of dwelling on what you need to eliminate, simply eat more of the good stuff so that it crowds out both the desire and the space for unhealthy foods.

Try not to be too rigid with yourself or others. People who are hard on themselves tend to be judgmental of others. That's counterproductive. If your mission to eat better becomes a strict chore and strains your relationships, it will make you miserable and longing for your old, comfortable ways. Remember what works for your body may not necessarily work for someone else's; that's bio-individuality.

How to Eat

Of course, I couldn't possibly lay down the rules of such a personal and elusive concept as "how to eat." Nevertheless, here are some helpful tips:

STAY NOURISHED: Stay on top of cravings by beginning the day with a sustaining breakfast and eating a nutritious lunch. Make lunch your largest meal of the day, and when possible eat dinner early and fairly light—a large salad or vegetarian option, for instance—so that you're not overeating close to bedtime. And keep hydrated all day by drinking water.

CHEW: Sounds obvious, but you'd be surprised how many people don't, at least not properly. Thorough mastication helps your body digest nutrients better. To see just how little chewing we all do, try chewing 10 to 20 times per mouthful or until the food becomes liquid—not easy, right?

EAT SLOWLY: Pause between bites to savor the flavors and check in with your stomach to ask it "are you full yet?" This will make your meal last longer and help to prevent the discomfort and weight gain associated with overeating.

DON'T OVEREAT: Eating slowly and chewing properly helps to prevent this, but note how much you order in the first place. Practice portion control. And realize that it's unnecessary to order an appetizer and dessert as well as an entrée. If you're still hungry after eating slowly, you can always order more. Have a light fruit snack before going out to eat; if you arrive at a restaurant starving, you're likely to overeat. And skip the bread at the beginning of the meal.

AVOID DISTRACTIONS: If you're not good at blocking out extraneous noise and distractions, you might want to eat in silence or alone occasionally. But given that most meals—especially in restaurants—

are a fun, shared experience, try to dine with people who don't give you indigestion. Keep heated debates to a minimum so that you can chew and assimilate the food properly. Reading and television are also distracting.

DON'T EAT UNDER STRESS: Anxiety and anger shut down the digestive function as part of the "fight or flight" response. Eating under such circumstances can cause indigestion. At such times you will be tempted to go for comfort foods or to overeat to numb your feelings. If you do arrive stressed at a restaurant, take a few deep breaths and remember your intention.

PRACTICE GRATITUDE: Be thankful for your food and for all the people and forces that brought it to your table: the sun that shone down on it, the farmer who grew it and the waiter who delivered it. Taking a moment to give thanks will calm you and remind you of your connection to the whole. It will also enable you to feel grateful for real, healthy food and simple pleasures.

ENJOY: Whatever you choose to eat—even if you know it is not perfectly healthy—allow yourself to enjoy it. Guilt is a stressor that makes you, and your digestive system, unhappy.

EXPERIMENT: It's that bio-individuality thing again. Experiment with different dietary theories and foods so that over time you can discover what works best for you and your body. At the very least, eat a few meals each week with no animal products by ordering proteins such as beans. Whatever you do, eat your veggies!

SOCIAL SITUATIONS
Even with the best intentions you will occasionally end up at a restaurant that does not serve healthy food and/or with a group of diners who do not share your dietary goals. What to do?

ORDER SIDES: Most restaurants have a selection of side dishes that you can create a meal out of, such as vegetables and a whole grain.

SPECIAL ORDER: An accommodating, creative chef will be happy to make something especially for you. Try requests like: "I know it's not on the menu, but could you put together a plate of vegetables and beans for me?" or "I'd like an extra-large version of your side salad as my entrée."

SKIP THE FREEBIES: Just because the bread is complimentary does not mean that you have to eat it. Likewise, try to ignore those fortune cookies or mints that arrive with the bill.

ASK FOR SAUCE ON THE SIDE: If the salad dressings and sauces are not up to par, ask for the waitstaff to bring them on the side so that you can monitor how much you use.

ASK FOR SUBSTITUTIONS: Some restaurants charge for doing this, and some don't. In any case, it is worth asking for things like green veggies or even boiled potatoes instead of french fries.

I hope to have left you with enough inspiration, motivation and education to put my five precepts into action. It's time to start enjoying your food more than ever while getting healthier at the same time. You *can* have your naturally sweetened dessert and eat it too. So let's get to the best part (I have a feeling you may have taken a peek already) and check out the restaurants.

THE RESTAURANTS

Icon Key

Meals for 1 (including beverage, tax, and tip) under $10

$11–$30

$31–$60

Above $60

Vegetarian menu

Primarily meat-based menu

Vegan menu

Raw menu

Gluten-free options

Naturally sweetened desserts

Nearby subways

4FOOD
New American, Fast Food
286 Madison Ave. (40th St.)
Ⓢ ④ ⑤ ⑥ ⑦
212 810-4592
4food.com
Mon–Fri: 7am–11pm

Remember studying in advance for tests in school? Apply that logic to eating at 4Food, a midtown restaurant that is devoted to taking the junk out of fast food.

There are seven steps to compiling your healthy dream burger (or salad/rice bowl) including buns, donut-shaped patties, veggie scoops, cheese, and toppings. We recommend you check out the ingredient list before you arrive to simplify the ordering process. Adventurous first-time visitors might dive right in to mixing and matching, while others, intimidated by the sheer volume of choices, might prefer to choose from existing customer favorites. Ordering can be done on the web, in-house by iPad, or the old-fashioned way, right at the counter.

I chose the latter, and glad I did, as the face of the helpful staff let me know when I was onto something delicious. When I combined a wild salmon patty on a pumpernickel bun with red cabbage slaw, avocado, and garlic mayo, I received an enthusiastic head nod. After selecting a salad bowl of sharp radicchio and spinach topped with lamb skewers, goat cheese, and a basil pesto, eyes lit up. I grew more adventurous, pairing a multigrain bun and turkey patty with avocado and mango chipotle pepper sauce, a topping that brought a welcome zing to the oft-boring turkey burger. Classic burger lovers can stick to a beef burger with cheddar, pickles, lettuce, and tomato—or elevate this simple combination with a dash of mango hot sauce. Veggie lovers can choose from a long list of 'veggiescoops' that include Chinese-braised kale, asparagus, mushrooms, and roasted brussels sprouts. An unsweetened green tea washed down my burger, and for once, walking out of a fast food joint I felt nourished yet treated by decadent ingredients.

Noting a dry pumpernickel bun and under-seasoned salmon patty, 4food receives a B+ from me.   JESSICA COLLEY

In the unofficially unnamed grey zone west of Soho and north of Tribeca stands 508, a loungy restaurant (on the ground floor of the building RENT was supposedly written in and about). Finding impressive under-the-radar restaurants in NYC is close to impossible, so we were thrilled to find this unknown diamond in the rough.

The rectangular restaurant opens like a garage onto the street, as sleek as the stacks of books that line the wall. At the bar, patrons slurp oysters and sip well-crafted cocktails and locally made ales from 508's own brewpub. Married partners Anderson Sant'anna and Jennifer Hill run the sustainably-minded kitchen. All the meats on the menu are hormone- and antibiotic-free, and the menu changes (albeit only slightly) with the seasons. The one shortcoming of their sustainable menu: most of the artisanal cheeses are from the old country (we would have liked to have seen a few local cheese makers).

The menu is slightly chaotic, placing a Spanish-style morcilla blood sausage next to platters of babaganoush. Small plates are the bulk of the offerings, though there are salads, fresh pastas, and half a dozen entrees as well. Our salad of roasted beets, greens, and goat cheese was plentiful and satisfying. The pastas are made in-house daily, but the roasted duck, Brussels sprouts, goat cheese, and pine nuts over spinach fettuccini tasted muddled and lacked focus. The entrees impressed us; hanger steak with horseradish mashed potatoes and bitter Swiss chard hit all the right notes, as did an interesting arrangement of lamb chops with pea gnocchi, pancetta, and hazelnuts. Nevermind the few missteps, 508's stylishly sustainable plates and posh setting are enough to place this unnamed neighborhood firmly on my map.

SCARLETT LINDEMAN

508
New American, Mediterranean
508 Greenwich St. (@ Spring St.)
1 **C** **E**
212 219-2444
508nyc.com
Mon–Wed: 11am–12am,
Thu–Fri: 11am–2am,
Sat: 5pm–2am,
Sun: 11am–12am

ABC KITCHEN
New American
35 E. 18th St. (Broadway &
Park Ave South)

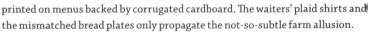

212 475-5829
abckitchennyc.com
Mon–Wed: 12pm–3pm,
    5:30pm–10:30pm,
Thu: 12pm–3pm, 5:30pm–11pm,
Fri: 12pm–3pm, 5:30pm–11:30pm,
Sat: 11am–3:30pm, 5:30pm–11:30pm,
Sun: 11am–3:30pm, 5:30pm–10pm

The sustainably-minded furnishing store ABC Carpet and Home has come together with prolific restaurateur Jean-Georges Vongerichten to bring eco-friendly food to the forefront of gourmet dining. The restaurant is attached to the store, so patrons can peruse racks of organic linens then retire to the restaurant for organic and locally sourced foods with classic Jean-Georges flair.

The whitewashed dining room with exposed wooden beams is distinctly reminiscent of a barn, and dishes like pretzel-dusted calamari, heirloom bean salads and roasted fiddlehead ferns are

printed on menus backed by corrugated cardboard. The waiters' plaid shirts and the mismatched bread plates only propagate the not-so-subtle farm allusion.

Gimmickry aside, the food is outstanding. Executive chef Dan Kluger runs a smooth kitchen with brilliant offerings. The description of the roasted carrot and avocado salad bored us, but the carrots came caramelized with sprouts, greens, a tasty curry spice and a hint of heat. Our pleasantly charred whole-wheat pizza crust performed beautifully under spinach, herbs, and goat cheese. Black sea bass was subtly perfumed with chilies, mint, and herbs while red bliss potatoes bobbed in the flavorful broth. Juicy chicken breast with perfectly crispy skin was elevated by lightly pickled escarole under velvety mashed potatoes, and the Akaushi cheeseburger with herbed mayo and fries are solid (if unimaginative).

The only missteps were a whole-wheat pasta bigoli with a flaccid pork ragu and the lack of local beef—it's flown in from Texas. If you don't have time for a three-course farm-to-table feast, drop by the adjacent café for housemade sodas with basil and mint or an organic smoothie with blue-green algae and bee pollen.

ABC Kitchen stands at an intersection of upscale dining and sustainable credibility: though the consciousness can be forced, it's easy to ignore when the food is this fine.   SCARLETT LINDEMAN

"Whole foods." "Slow foods." The words are thrown around with abandon these days. Happily enough, there's a little place in the East Village that gets both pretty much just right. Angelica Kitchen has been serving organic, vegan, Asian-inflected cuisine since 1976—long before it was trendy.

ANGELICA KITCHEN
Gourmet Vegan
300 E. 12th St. @ 2nd Ave.
L 6 R
212 228-2909
angelicakitchen.com
Daily: 11:30 am–10:30 pm
Cash only, BYOB

One caveat about the eatery: It gets packed, and it doesn't take reservations. Would-be diners must wait on a cushy seat in the foyer, eyeballing the rows of light wooden tables and hoping one becomes available. The fare is worth the wait, however. A fragrant bowl of "dashi and noodle" (a simple Japanese broth with soba noodles) swirls with seaweed, fresh ginger, soy sauce and silky shiitakes. Spoon up flavorful bites and savor the notion that everything is organic, most ingredients are fairly traded and sourced from small local farms, and extra food is donated to City Harvest. Take a sip of water—it's filtered here; in a pro-environment move, Angelica refuses to use bottles—and skip slightly bland vegetable sushi in favor of a simple "dragon bowl" of rice, beans, tofu, greens and a tangle of mineral-packed sea vegetables. The dish seems bland at first, but gains traction once various sauces are applied: "Gravy" based in a simple brown rice roux lends tofu a welcome spiciness, and brown rice becomes much more interesting under a drizzle of fresh carrot-ginger dressing. Angelica's broad menu features two gourmet vegan specials daily in addition to naturally sweetened, dairy-free desserts. Though fruit crumbles were nothing to write home about, we loved a delicate mint custard in a crunchy oat tart shell. A small Angelica outpost next door offers both savories and sweets "to go"—and since both have rabid followers, it's worth even carnivores giving Angelica a shot.

ALEX VAN BUREN

AURORA RISTORANTE
Italian
510 Broome St. (W. Broadway and
Thompson St.) ① Ⓐ Ⓒ Ⓔ
212 334-9020
auroraristorante.com
Mon–Thu: 12pm–11pm,
Fri: 12pm–12am,
Sat: 11am–12am,
Sun: 11am–10pm

Shopping is so exhausting. Thank goodness, then—for those loaded up with H&M and Calvin Klein bags—that an excellent modern Italian trattoria is esconced in Soho. Aurora is a comfort from the moment one walks in its door. The hostess greets diners with a wide smile. Hanging tin lamps and exposed brick walls induce Old World nostalgia. The charming waiter will have a velvety, aromatic glass of biodynamic Barbera d'Alba in your hand within minutes. The wine matched beautifully with the best starter we tried—sweet coils of roasted fennel and savory homemade Berkshire pork sausage, a perfect counterpoint to mouth-puckering (and good-for-you) organic dandelion greens. The *primi* may even outshine the *secondi* here, especially a generous portion of penne mingling with hearty chunks of eggplant, grape tomatoes and luscious pieces of buffalo mozzarella that could fool an Italian grandma.

We were pleased to spy even more local sourcing in entrées: Hudson Valley-raised duck breast was rosy and crisp-skinned, and paired with a duck leg to fight over. Vegetarians and pescatarians can partake in either of numerous meat-free pasta dishes or the fishy fare dotting the menu, like a moist, flaky slab of halibut tucked into parchment paper along with slices of lemon and a dusting of herbs (though we could do without the overcooked scallions served alongside them, advertised as "caramelized," but served rather burnt). That said, many gems are to be found on this menu, and we'd return in a heartbeat, particularly for the wallet-friendly pasta. One caveat: Though the atmosphere is charming—exposed pipes lend a modern edge to the otherwise rustic interior—less-than-stellar acoustics and tightly placed tables make this a late-in-the-relationship, not early, sort of date place.

ALEX VAN BUREN

It's the flagship restaurant of clog-wearing, orange-haired TV chef Mario Batali's empire. It's arguably the best-known Italian restaurant in Gotham. It is still among the hardest reservations in town to snag. And it was news to us that Molto Mario is a huge fan of sourcing local and sustainably raised fare.

BABBO RISTORANTE E ENOTECA
Italian
110 Waverly Pl.
(6th Ave. & Macdougal St.)
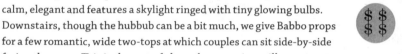
212 777-0303
babbonyc.com
Mon: 5:30pm–11:15pm,
Tue–Sat: 11:30am–1:30, 5:30pm–11:15pm,
Sun: 5pm–10:45pm

At Babbo, Batali's West Village eatery, push by the tourists and head to a table upstairs: The second tier of the split-level space is calm, elegant and features a skylight ringed with tiny glowing bulbs. Downstairs, though the hubbub can be a bit much, we give Babbo props for a few romantic, wide two-tops at which couples can sit side-by-side facing the room. This is the sort of place where a waiter will re-cover your tablecloth with a precisely placed napkin moments after you've dripped sauce on the table—something missing at Batali's excellent but chill little sister, Lupa—pleasing those who like their waitstaff on the attentive side.

Antipasti, *primi*, *secondi*, *contorni*, and *dolce*—the staples of fine Italian fare—are all accounted for. Vegetarians can dine fairly well here, with several meat-free pasta dishes on the menu and a smattering of vegetable antipasti. Choose carefully: A platter of artichokes proved crunchy, and we wished we'd ordered the fluffy arugula salad that floated to another table. Of the pastas, we weren't crazy for organic lamb-stuffed "love letters," a signature dish, but found eggy pappardelle noodles snaking through a rich red ragú to be a worthy take on the classic. Entrées likewise impressed, especially a leggy, tender organic quail propped primly on sticks of salsify with a drizzle of *saba* (a grape *jus*). We'll return here, tourists be damned, to nosh our way through the menu—it, like the chef himself, is epic. ALEX VAN BUREN

BACK FORTY WEST

New American

70 Prince St. (@ Crosby St.)

Ⓝ Ⓡ Ⓑ Ⓓ Ⓕ Ⓜ ⑥

212 219-8570

Mon–Thu: 8:30am–3pm,
    5:30pm–10:30pm,
Fri: 8:30am–3pm, 5:30pm–11pm,
Sat: 11am–3pm, 5:30pm–11pm,
Sun: 11am–6pm

BACK FORTY

190 Ave. B (@ 12th St.) Ⓛ

212 388-1990

Mon–Thu: 6pm–11pm,
Fri: 6pm–12am,
Sat: 11am–3pm, 6pm–12am,
Sun: 11am–3:30pm, 6pm–10pm
backfortynyc.com

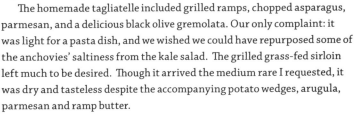

Back Forty West has revived Savoy's long shuttered location on Soho's Prince Street. What appears to be a tiny café from the outside actually houses a casual and elegant two-story, full-service restaurant within. Pale yellow walls, exposed brick, and warm lighting combine to emit a cozy country energy.

The menu is unconventionally organized by eating utensil: Breads, Hands, Spoon & Ladle, Fork, Fork & Knife, and Spoon. While it's evident that the Spoon-only section is reserved for dessert, expect to find sides, appetizers, and entrees interspersed amongst each other.

The grilled kale and escarole salad (found in the Fork section) appeared in a large wooden bowl mixed with creamy parmesan dressing, white anchovies, fried capers, and crispy chickpeas. While the grilled kale was a bit salty, the soft and savory texture combined with the raw, crunchy escarole in an unconventional way. The crunch of the capers and chickpeas were a welcome addition to an already innovative salad.

The homemade tagliatelle included grilled ramps, chopped asparagus, parmesan, and a delicious black olive gremolata. Our only complaint: it was light for a pasta dish, and we wished we could have repurposed some of the anchovies' saltiness from the kale salad. The grilled grass-fed sirloin left much to be desired. Though it arrived the medium rare I requested, it was dry and tasteless despite the accompanying potato wedges, arugula, parmesan and ramp butter.

The smoked Catskill trout however, was the standout dish of the night. Light and flavorful, the dish continually entertained our palates with the saffron-braised artichokes, English peas and dill. While a few dishes may require some tweaking, Back Forty West does succeed in creating wholesome and comforting dishes made with fresh, local ingredients. AMY SUNG

Balaboosta adopts the trans-cultural practice of placing a beloved's portrait in its lived-in, homey dining room; the white brick wall's sole decoration is an illuminated picture of the balaboosta herself. She watches over us as we taste the recipes she dutifully passed to her niece (chef Einat Admony): the expression on her face urging and confident but never smug.

BALABOOSTA
Mediterranean
214 Mulberry St. (Prince St. & Spring St.) ⑥ Ⓑ Ⓓ Ⓕ Ⓜ
212 966-7366
balaboostanyc.com
Mon: 5:30pm–11pm
Tue–Thu: 12am–3pm, 5:30pm–11pm,
Fri: 12pm–3pm, 5:30pm–11:30pm,
Sat: 11am–3pm, 5:30pm–11:30pm,
Sun: 11am–3pm, 5:30pm–10:00pm

The chef's immortalized aunt has every reason to be proud of her small plates. The interactive hummus requires a little muscle from an elected table member. A few unmashed chickpeas pierce the top of the concoction, which arrives in a mortar and pestle for diners to pulverize to their desired consistency. However you slice (er, squash) it, this creamy, lemony hummus is probably the best I've ever tried. Falafel (which hails from Chef Admony's Taïm) forms a protective shell around grass-fed beef clusters accompanied by a cool, tangy tahini dip, and the smallish pizza competently balances sweet carrot puree and caramelized onions and savory goat cheese and cilantro.

Chef Admony's entrees, though good, could benefit from some of her aunt's posthumous tweaking. Chicken under a brick succeeds in the golden-crisp exterior department, but its white meat could have been a little juicier. Fettuccine also suffers from the "just decent" affliction (not a bad one to have, mind you); the light pasta's vegetables (save the overcooked fava beans) are crisp—though not flavorful enough to coat the wide noodles. Despite these nit-picky complaints, I still managed to obediently clean my plate and elicit an approving glance from the dining room's saintly matriarch.   ALLIX GENESLAW

BARBUTO
Italian, New American
775 Washington St. (@ W. 12th St.)
(A) (C) (E) (L) (1) (2)
212 924-9700
barbutonyc.com
Mon–Wed: 12pm–4:30pm,
    5:30pm–11pm
Thu–Fri: 12pm–4:30pm, 5:30pm–12am,
Sat: 12pm–3:30pm, 5:30pm–12am,
Sun: 12pm–3:30pm, 5:30pm–10pm

Jonathan Waxman is a California native and former head chef of Alice Waters' Chez Panisse, largely considered the epicenter of the local-organic food movement. So it comes as no surprise that his restaurant, Barbuto, boasts a casual West Coast vibe and makes use of fresh, seasonal ingredients.

We arrived on a warm California-esque evening; diners spilled out onto Washington and West 12th Streets through the open

garage door, and Waxman milled about the open kitchen, tasting and sipping. His approachability extends to the Italy-meets-California menu; it changes daily and emphasizes simple preparations like pan-roasting and grilling in the handsome wood-burning brick oven. We began with a straightforward, yet satisfyingly crunchy crudi of seasonal shaved vegetables (firm asparagus, radish and carrot) tossed in breadcrumbs and a peppery anchovy-pecorino dressing. The silky linguine that arrived next also touted seasonality: ramps, with their leafy tops and onion-flavored roots, mingled nicely with generous slices of garlic and jalapeno. After the slightly spicy pasta, Waxman's famous roast chicken proved a pleasantly herbal, slightly sweet transition; its crispy grilled skin was dressed in a fragrant salsa verde of tarragon, sage, parsley and capers. We paired the moist bird with a side of broccoli rabe sautéed in garlic and chilies, another simple preparation that showcased a vegetable's freshness and flavor. While roast chicken is perhaps Barbuto's most celebrated entrée, we were just as taken with the substantial, very juicy Hampshire pork chop. It was served with a tart rhubarb mostarda flavored with citrus and spice, along with large slices of crisp radish and fennel. The pungency of each vegetable served with the chop somehow shone through, evidence of Waxman's California philosophy: seasonal produce needs no fussing over, especially when it's exceptionally fresh.   SARAH AMANDOLARE

Smack dab in the middle of NYU territory stands BareBurger, a gleaming restaurant that has hungry students and Manhattanites chomping down on burgers and organic fries. It's a bright and lively follow-up to their successful Queens original.

BAREBURGER
American
Multiple Locations (see website)
bareburger.com

The menu abounds with choice, so your carb-free, vegetarian, sustainable carnivore and adventurous foodie friends will all find something to enjoy. There are nine different burgers and a few specials. You have a choice of brioche, 7-grain bun, wrap, or a lettuce wrap; the burger from beef, turkey, chicken, veggie, portabella mushroom, bison, elk, or ostrich; and also from slew of cheeses, toppings, fries, and condiments including organic ketchup. Little touches like agave nectar for sweetening, multiple dipping sauces, and a kid's menu show that BareBurger is eager to please.

The Original BareBurger is made from Piedmontese beef with a thin mantle of cheese, iceberg lettuce, tomato, red onion, and "special sauce." Though delicious, I'd recommend the more interesting options. A spicy bacon elk burger drips with juice and flavor while even the veggie burger is an especially moist patty of grains, legumes, and buttery avocado.

If utensils are more your style (not to mention a good way to get your greens), there are a handful of salads on the menu. A baby arugula, pepperjack cheese, avocado, and walnut salad was a little underdressed but could make a meal with all of the fixings.

Take caution; it is easy to overindulge—remember, an organic milkshake is still a milkshake. Nevertheless, if you are going for the burger, fries, and shake trinity, then it may as well be at a luscious, organic, eco-conscious restaurant that has low-energy toilets and walls lined with repurposed wood. It's great guilt-free fast food worth braving the NYU crowds for.   SCARLETT LINDEMAN

BELL BOOK AND CANDLE
New American
141 W. 10th St. (6th & 7th Ave.)
(A)(B)(C)(D)(E)(F)(M)(1)(2)(3)
212 414-2355
bbandcnyc.com
Mon–Wed: 5:30pm–10:30pm,
Thu–Sat: 5:30pm–11pm,
Sun: 11:30am–3:30pm,
     5:30pm–10:30pm

The intriguing atmosphere inside Bell Book & Candle, an eatery nearly hidden beneath West 10th Street, makes it easy to forget what's overhead: an equally beguiling rooftop aeroponic garden. Numerous vegetables and herbs are grown onsite for use in the restaurant, the cherry on top of an impressively sustainable operation. Filtered water is bottled on site, gobs of local cheeses are on offer, and fruit-centric cocktails even tout unexpected additions like fig jam or roasted pear puree.

The rooftop mixed greens, one of the restaurant's living leaf salads, made for a refreshing start. Arriving in concentric circles of buttery bibb lettuce, subtly spicy varieties of arugula and bits of frisee, it was finished with crisp cucumbers, firm grape tomatoes and a delicately sweet thousand island dressing. House-made burrata arrived next; soft and mild on its own, it proved a perfect counterpoint to sweet and charcoal-blistered tomatoes, diced garlic and ramps. Although Bell Book & Candle takes sustainability seriously, the décor is playfully literary—newspaper clippings about Dylan Thomas and Charles Bukowski along with scattered sculpture and kooky wallpaper lighten the main dining room's exposed brick and dark wood. Drunken bean dip echoed the lighthearted vibe, with mellow pinto beans and spicy chorizo doused in Pork Slap beer, a slightly ginger-flavored ale.

Although intent on making the most of seasonal produce, the restaurant doesn't hold back on proteins: two grilled lamb chops were delightfully juicy, slicked with a lemon, oregano and olive oil glaze that sharpened the meat's soft gaminess. Other meats, including grilled hanger steak and organic "gin & tonic" salmon, were similarly moist and toothsome. Both came with the sort of accompaniments that were memorable themselves: a smooth acidic lime emulsion with the salmon and creamily potent blue cheese with the steak. Sides like these elevate what are already superb entrees, reiterating the menu's uncommon depth. 　　　　　SARAH AMANDOLARE

You may know chef Guy Vaknin from Gordon Ramsey's "Hell's Kitchen", but he's since retired his meat and fish knives to sling 100% vegan food at his restaurant, Beyond Sushi. Those sick of traditional California and vegetable rolls can try Vaknin's innovative, fishless sushi featuring fresh vegetables, fruits, and nutritious black rice or six-grain rice.

Maintaining high standards for freshness, all items are made-to-order and are quite labor intensive. We watched as Vaknin attentively trained his staff, cueing reminders that the carrot-ginger dressing paired with the crunchy pickled gobo, carrot, daikon and avocado roll. Overseeing the careful construction of our Spicy Mang, Vaknin shaped black rice into a perfect rectangle and rolled it with rainbow rows of ripe avocado, mango, and crisp cucumber strips. A spicy cabbage, pepper, and carrot mixture was lovingly draped over the roll without mangling the shape. A true pioneer, Vaknin thoughtfully packages his custom sauces for to-go customers in plastic tubes that look like they come straight out of a chem lab. The innovative packaging kept the creamy, tofu-based dressing separate during transportation and was easy to dispense—we didn't even need soy sauce.

True to its name, if sushi isn't your game, gluten-free rice paper wraps, rice bed salads and fresh juices are also available. We were surprised to find the seemingly simple wraps anything but ordinary. The delightfully chewy, sticky exterior was fun to eat and contained delicious Asian combinations like a flavorful, nutty soba salad with carrot batons, jalapeno peanut butter, crushed peanuts and sesame oil, balanced with cilantro and a sweet soy mirin glaze.

As we stared at our beautifully arranged to-go container, we almost felt bad eating these gorgeous works of art—until we discovered these beauties taste just as good as they look. CHELSEA GRANT

BEYOND SUSHI
Japanese, Fast Food
229 E. 14th St. (2nd & 3rd Ave.)
④ ⑤ ⑥ Ⓛ Ⓝ Ⓠ Ⓡ
646 861-2889
beyondsushinyc.com
Sun-Wed: 11:30am-10pm,
Thu-Sat: 11:30am-11pm

THE GREEN ROLL
75 9th Ave. (@ Chelsea Market)
① ② ③ Ⓐ Ⓒ Ⓔ Ⓛ
212 929-2889
Mon–Sat: 10am–8pm,
Sun: 10am–7:30pm

BIRRERIA (EATALY)

Italian, Austrian, German
200 Fifth Ave. (@ 23rd St.)

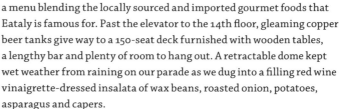

N R F M 4 6

212 937-8910
eatalyny.com
Mon–Wed: 11:30am–10pm,
Thu–Sat: 11:30am–11pm,
Sun: 11:30am–10pm

Since opening in late 2010, Flatiron's massive Italian food emporium, Eataly, has become one of the city's most tempting destinations. Still somehow—as if aisles upon aisles of specialty items, fresh produce and six full-service restaurants wasn't alluring enough—Batali and the Bastianichs have upped the ante even further by debuting a 4,500-sq. foot brewery and restaurant on the roof.

Far from your typical brews and brats beer garden, Birreria is a rooftop oasis featuring artisanal house-crafted ales and a menu blending the locally sourced and imported gourmet foods that Eataly is famous for. Past the elevator to the 14th floor, gleaming copper beer tanks give way to a 150-seat deck furnished with wooden tables, a lengthy bar and plenty of room to hang out. A retractable dome kept wet weather from raining on our parade as we dug into a filling red wine vinaigrette-dressed insalata of wax beans, roasted onion, potatoes, asparagus and capers.

Detailing farms and meat purveyors, the menu boasts flavorful grilled dishes like fat-marbled Donley Ranch skirt steak elevated by salsa verde, and a succulent salt-encrusted Pennsylvania chicken thigh with sweet corn, purslane and olive-almond pesto sauce (the night's standout). If you're craving more traditional beer garden fare, don't overlook the housemade sausages, especially a savory and sweet Emilia Romagna-inspired ground pork link spiced with warm clove and nutmeg. Vegetarians will delight in hearty mushroom entrées. We sampled whole roasted maitakes atop a bed of rich pecorino sardo crema, and sides like braised cabbage and pickled vegetables are excellent accompaniments.

To wash it down, choose from three unfiltered, unpasteurized and naturally carbonated ales brewed on-site, nine Italian and American draft microbrews, more than 30 bottled beers and select wines on tap. Plan ahead for a coveted dinner reservation, then sit back, relax and say Ciao to a roof-raising good time.   MEGAN MURPHY

Vegan and raw-foods restaurants sometimes have a formal, slightly sterile air: "Healthy food is on the premises!" It can be tricky to relax. This is not a problem at Blossom—particularly at its downtown location. The split-level, modern space is decked out with slim Japanese screens, ethereal curtains and pretty windowside tables, making it utterly dateworthy.

Several different regions of the world see a brief spin in the limelight, such as the American South, making a cameo in an excellently crisp cake of potatoes and black-eyed peas in a puddle of sweetly spicy chipotle aioli. An Italian tip of the hat comes via delicate ravioli floating in cashew cream flecked with sage and sautéed wild mushrooms. A Brazilian twist on tempeh finds it roasted in a savory stew of black beans spiked with orange. Avoid not-so-healthy wheat gluten (seitan) in favor of other options like two rounds of flavorful lentils, stacked and snug in a flaky phyllo crust and served on a tangle of sweet caramelized onions. Of the naturally sweetened desserts occasionally on offer, we loved a silky lavender tartlet sprinkled with über-fresh blueberries.

Uptown, Café Blossom serves a nearly identical menu with the addition of lunch offerings in a space lighter on the romance. A slim, efficient banquette wends its way down one side behind a sleek bar. Stop in for a quick bite like a tasty banana-berry shake or a hefty bowl of divinely creamy butternut squash soup. Those seeking heartier fare should stick to dinner entrées (superior on our visit to a messy hummus-and-salsa-topped veggie burger). The best were sweet potato gnocchi, served to delightful effect on a pile of jewel-toned golden and chioggia beets. Overall, we found the Blossoms a fine way to introduce naysayers to gourmet vegan cuisine at its finest.   ALEX VAN BUREN

BLOSSOM
Gourmet Vegan
187 Ninth Ave. (21st & 22nd St.)
①ⒸⒺ
212 627-1144
blossomnyc.com
Mon–Thu: 12pm–2:45pm, 5pm–9:30pm,
Fri–Sat: 12pm–2:45pm, 5pm–10pm,
Sun: 12pm–2:45pm, 5pm–9pm

CAFÉ BLOSSOM
Multiple locations (see website)
blossomcafe.com

BLOSSOM DU JOUR
Multiple locations (see website)
blossomdujour.com

BLUE HILL
New American
75 Washington Pl. (6th Ave. &
Washington Square Park)
① Ⓐ Ⓒ Ⓔ Ⓑ Ⓓ Ⓕ Ⓜ
212 539-1776
bluehillnyc.com
Mon–Sat: 5pm–11pm,
Sun: 5pm–10pm

Dan Barber's farm-to-table motif is so coyly self-aware it's almost cartoonlike. Witness the "carrots on the fence" *amuse-bouche* at his Village eatery Blue Hill, in which carrots arrive impaled on a nail-studded slab of wood and trailing long emerald fronds. Diners sit, and stare, and when Bugs Bunny does not materialize they pluck the carrots from their wires, marveling at the simple glaze of aged balsamic vinegar that causes carrot to taste, if possible, more like itself.

The space is elegant and serene, with cushy red chairs and banquettes lining the walls, and the staff was perhaps the most charming we encountered—ideal conditions for traipsing through a menu chock-full of local, seasonal, organic ingredients. Barber helped found this trend, and his mastery of it shines both in an end-of-summer tomato salad layered with grilled peaches and swirled with ricotta, and to-die-for sweet corn ravioli. A sherry vinegar-brown butter sauce drips from bites of pasta concealing earthy pumpkin and explosively sweet corn—Indian Summer in a single bite.

Our female sommelier was a genius, expertly matching a stellar organic Spanish white wine with nearly rare sashimi-style cobia laid over a bed of crunchy macadamia nuts and diced zucchini. Even better was a plush leg of Vermont-sourced baby lamb, sitting pretty along with a smattering of buttery wild mushrooms in a wine-drenched jus. Those who must indulge in sugar might do so here: A spoonful of raspberry jam nestles inside a dark chocolate shell, arriving in a river of "milk jam"— coconut milk, milk and vanilla mingling in one sweet bite. All dairy comes straight from Barber's farm upstate, the locale of his other eatery.

Cynics might think such a wonderful place couldn't possibly be run by a down-to-earth, charming guy. We didn't think to ask when we saw him laughing with a friend before dinner, preparing to take his dog for a walk.

ALEX VAN BUREN

Enter this eclectic townhouse from the bottom up, its basement entrance a bashful segue into its stacked dining room levels. Each offers a different vibe—a back bar with funky zig-zag stripes and unpainted wooden tables, a bohemian living room embellished with mismatched picture frames and an antique

BOBO RESTAURANT
New American
181 W. 10th St. (@ 7th Ave. South)
① Ⓐ Ⓒ Ⓔ Ⓑ Ⓓ Ⓕ Ⓜ
212 488-2626
bobonyc.com
Mon: 6pm–10pm, Tue–Wed: 6pm–11pm,
Th–Fr: 5pm–12am, Sat: 12pm–12am,
Sun: 12pm–10pm

candelabra, and a relaxed outdoor patio dotted with dangling potted plants and simple white latticework (if it's nice out, opt for the latter).

The food, each dish more solid than the next, knows exactly where it stands. Chicken can often arrive dry and tasteless, but the Bobo chicken turned the bird's bad rap on its feathery head—its juiciness made me question what protein I was consuming. Its crispy skin and unexpectedly spicy sauce has become the standard for all other poultry I've tasted since. Also simple and reliable are the beef and trout entrees. Sirloin, served in strips, is accompanied by tender fingerlings and a velvety leek puree that mimicked the taste and texture of whipped potatoes. Though classically prepared and presented, the trout, whose mild flaky flesh whitens beautifully toward the edges, is made unique with an intense Meyer lemon dip and leafy purslane.

Veggie sides and thimble-sized canapes are a fun addition to the main courses, providing bite-sized palate teasers. My favorite was the Peking duck, presented with micro cilantro, sriracha-infused mayonnaise, and pickled radishes to fill the swiss chard leaves that replace the traditional flour pancakes. The chef sources locally, preparing a tasty heirloom tomato side from the Brooklyn Grange rooftop farm. The lemon subtly resurfaces in the Caesar-like dressing beneath the battered zucchini blossom and Swiss chard canapes. After such a successful meal, the restaurant's classification—cool, yuppie, whatever—is irrelevant. The only label that resonates with me is the one associated with the food: delicious.   ALLIX GENESLAW

BOULEY

French

163 Duane St. (Hudson St.)

① ② ③ ④ ⑤ ⑥ Ⓐ Ⓒ Ⓔ

212 964-2525

davidbouley.com

Mon–Sat: 11:30am–11:30pm

From the first step into Bouley's gorgeous, classically decorated interior, diners are extracted from their fast-paced, gritty New York experience and transplanted to a serene, idyllic retreat. Luxurious velvet covers chairs and chaises and even frames picturesque landscape paintings; background noise, save the celebratory clink of champagne flutes and waiters' lulled menu explanations, is more or less nonexistent. The heightened elegance does require some acclimation (slouching and frantic texting, both characteristic of my usual behavior, suddenly felt unbecoming).

I had no trouble adjusting to the delicious food, of course. Heirloom tomato and roasted asparagus appetizers are both quintessentially French, perched atop cream-infused sauces. Thin, light cream is muddled with the red, yellow, and orange tomatoes' juicy drippings, while a thicker, more decadent base supports roasted asparagus. The chewy, truffle-studded gnocchi that surround the skinless, all-natural Pennsylvania chicken slices are equally rich. An emerald green chive sauce is drizzled throughout the dish, lending a surprisingly sweet flavor to the otherwise savory components. The Long Island duckling arrived with much anticipation—the excited waiters and neighboring table sung its praises—and immediately managed to elicit toothy grins from the two of us. The duckling's meat was a little more resilient than its fully-grown relative, but no matter—combined with its fatty casing and robust, mahogany jus, it delivered an impressive amount of flavor. Bok choy came on the side, upping the meal's green veggie quota and thereby delighting Jared.

Though such a pampering session was fleeting, I felt sufficiently satisfied and relaxed—that blissful smile was still plastered across my face as I was hurled back into the bustling Tribeca streets.

ALLIX GENESLAW

In the dining deserts of Midtown where chains are the norm and restaurants are often mobbed by the theatre-going crowd, it can be a hunt to find a sprig of organic arugula. Thankfully, there is Brickyard Gastropub, a restaurant on 9th Avenue trying to offer something a little more sustainable and a lot better.

BRICKYARD GASTROPUB
American
785 Ninth Ave (52nd St. & 53rd St.)
1 **A** **C** **E** **D**
212-767-0077
brickyardnyc.com
Daily: 11am–4am

During lunchtime, four different games play out on flatscreen TVs staggered across the room. Men in crisp button-downs lean over grass-fed burgers with Hudson Valley cheddar, slipping in an Ommegang Witte beer or two before heading back to their cubicles. The gastropub prides itself in pairing craft ales with their food—suggested pairings, often local brews, are listed on the menu.

Midday, there are salads and sandwiches, including a couple of bar snacks, like crab cake sliders with lemon-caper remoulade. They were so plump with crabmeat we happily ate them bun-less. Salads are bountifully meal-sized, especially when bolstered with perfectly cooked chicken or beef still steaming from the grill. A generic-sounding mandarin spinach salad packed the plate with bouncy spinach leaves, feta crumbles, red onion, and sweet orange segments that were much tastier than any we've ever had. An organic heirloom tomato and marinated fennel salad with pickled cucumber had the right idea but was a little too acidic, even for this vinegar lover.

There is a classically good portobello panini which sandwiches roasted peppers, eggplant, goat cheese in herbed focaccia from Amy's Bread and, like the aforementioned burger, it's served with addictive sweet potato fries (or salad if you prefer). After 5pm, the menu expands to include mussels steamed in white wine, pan seared mint crusted NY state lamb (among other sustainably raised meat entrees), and lots of vegetable sides. No need to settle for a cookie-cutter meal; Brickyard Gastropub is a step above the standards.   SCARLETT LINDEMAN

BRINKLEY'S
New American, British
406 Broome St. (@ Centre St.)
⑥ Ⓝ Ⓠ Ⓡ Ⓙ Ⓩ Ⓑ Ⓓ Ⓕ Ⓜ
212 680-5600
brinkleysnyc.com
Mon–Fri: 11am–2am,
Sat–Sun: 10am–2am

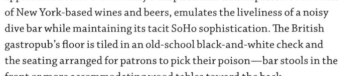

The booming, feel-good music of the Shins and the Foundations may make your fellow barfly or diner's witty comments nearly impossible to discern, but it's safe to assume that he or she is referring to either the ceiling's suspended blue bikes or the oversized diagram of a turtle's insides.

Brinkley's, with its polished approximation of T.G.I. Friday's-inspired flair and impressive selection of New York-based wines and beers, emulates the liveliness of a noisy dive bar while maintaining its tacit SoHo sophistication. The British gastropub's floor is tiled in an old-school black-and-white check and the seating arranged for patrons to pick their poison—bar stools in the front or more accommodating wood tables toward the back.

The menu options, like the bangers and mash, burger, and hot dog, may seem like run-of-the-mill bar food, but the inclusion of grass-fed meats and veggie accompaniments set this sustainable fare apart. Entree meats—the juicy grass-fed burger, sweet soy-addled ribs, and spicy sauerkraut-topped hot dog—come sans greens, so it's best to choose a vegetable plate or salad as a healthy addition. Sugar snap peas offer a pleasingly audible crunch, their sweetness offset by lightly bitter red onion but enhanced by a cool tomato dip. As for salads, the spinach and goat cheese option is perfectly dressed in a tangy honey vinaigrette, though beware: the cheese arrives as a dangerously delectable fried sphere. Also noteworthy are the meatballs, their alleged fame validated by the robust, chunky tomato sauce, pillowy interiors, and tasty sprinkling of parmesan and parsley. Brinkley's provides solid proof that scarfing sustainable, organic grub and late-night drinking needn't be mutually exclusive practices.

ALLIX GENESLAW

Maybe it's my Semitic upbringing, but the Yiddish term "bubby" conjures terrifying images of a chesty matron cloaked in an ill-fitting housedress, orthopedic slippers, and her own (hormone-filled) chicken soup recipe bravado. Bubby's menu, however, encouraged me to reevaluate my stringent definition of the word—barbecue, which is slow-smoked on the premises using local hogs and wood, is the porky specialty. A section of the menu lists its New York state sources and describes its pesticide-free and environmentally friendly allegiance.

BUBBY'S
American
120 Hudson St. (@ N. Moore St.)
① ② Ⓐ Ⓒ Ⓔ
212 219-0666
bubbys.com
Tue: 7am–12am,
Wed–Mon: Open 24 hrs.

The basin-sized barbecue sampler includes pulled pork, ribs, and a hot link and comes with two sides (sautéed spinach and baked beans, in our case). This meal is not for those who shy away from sodium; I fancy myself an ardent sodium fan and still clutched my naturally sweetened soda after each salty bite. Of the three piggy barbecue options, the pulled pork was my favorite—hot pepper flakes punctuated the sizable pile, giving it a nice degree of heat. The grass-fed burger, also mammoth in size, was cooked to a ruddy medium rare; its juices forming a beefy puddle for the crisp fries. The greens were equally plentiful and fresh. Spinach is delicious as a side or salad—the former is sautéed with ample amounts of garlic; the latter cool, crisp, and topped with thick-cut bacon. The buttermilk dressing (best ordered on the side) is sharp and milky, but if applied too liberally its gloppy consistency might overwhelm the vibrant greens. It seems I now have two bubbies to feed me till I'm incapacitated, though thankfully the latter employs ingredients that won't simultaneously fill my body with noxious chemicals.

ALLIX GENESLAW

BUVETTE
French, Tapas
42 Grove St. (Bedford & Bleecker St.)
Ⓐ Ⓑ Ⓒ Ⓓ Ⓔ Ⓕ Ⓜ ①
212 255-3590
ilovebuvette.com
Mon–Fri: 8am–2am,
Sat–Sun: 10am–2am

As we stepped into Buvette, we were greeted by a waiter donning a full-body apron over a crisp white shirt. The bakery-style bar to our left added to the French charm, and charcuterie plates were prepared next to specialty cocktails (all of which are served on silver platters) while small leather baskets on the bar held whole walnuts. A chalkboard of Italy and France with labeled wine regions hung on the brick wall, and a whimsical light sculpture of whisks and perforated shapes mimicking colanders by Warren Muller illuminated the long dining table in the back.

The menu is divided into tartinettes (crostinis), legumes (vegetables), viandes (meat), and poissons (seafood); all of the dishes are tapas sized. We started with the Pomodorini and Pesto di Parma tartinettes, served two to each plate atop crunchy sliced baguettes. The Pomodorini featured stracchino and sun-dried cherry tomatoes, and the Pesto di Parma was topped with proscuitto and a pesto-like mixture of parmesan and sage.

From the legumes, we especially loved the haricots verts: the crisp green beans and potatoes were perfectly highlighted by a tangy mustard vinaigrette. On the other hand, the beets were large and fresh but nothing special, and the artichokes were a bit too oily for our tastes.

The "Brandade de Morue", a house salt cod with olive oil, milk and garlic, was pureed to a smooth, spreadable consistency. The cod arrived cold in a mason jar with thinly sliced bread. Light but full of complex flavors, we devoured what we could and took the rest home to enjoy later.

For a charming atmosphere with sophisticated yet simple eats, stop into Buvette for small plates served with hints of France—all in the heart of the West Village.

AMY SUNG

The Village is stuffed with tasty bistros that are dimly lit and not too loud, and Café Cluny has followed in their date-friendly footsteps. In this romantic part of town, it is a comfort to find a spot where all the meat is antibiotic-free and organic, water is filtered and the produce is "either local or organic," as one waiter assured us. Though vegetarian and vegan options are scarce, omnivores should stop in, and keep an eye out for a smart prix-fixe intended to lure early birds.

CAFÉ CLUNY
American, French
284 W. 12th St.
(W. 4th & 8th Ave.)
Ⓐ Ⓒ Ⓔ Ⓛ ① ② ③ Ⓕ Ⓜ
212 255-6900
cafécluny.com
Mon: 8am–11pm,
Tue–Fri: 8am–12am,
Sat: 9am–12am,
Sun: 9am–11pm

The focus on whole foods is echoed by the assertive display of nature in the decor: Botanical prints line most walls, and even the bathroom, decked out with dried flowers and the like, feels oddly comforting. Little healthy touches may be missing—here again, there were no naturally sweetened desserts, and table salt seems to be just that, not sea—but service is sweet, and swift and the fare is fine. Yellowtail sashimi was fresh as could be, sparkling with sea salt and though a little predictably paired with grapefruit, given a nice herbal touch by a sprinkle of micro-celery greens. As for entrées, a juicy, thick steak was burnished with garlic-herb butter and slim, satisfyingly crunchy fries, and was superior to ruby medallions of duck. (Note that the chef sometimes errs on the rare side here, so inquire when you order.) The bird arrived with a delicious "crepe"—an odd little igloo of dough wrapped around sweet corn and duck confit—better than the entrée. If you must splurge on desserts, order either the Ronnybrook organic ice cream indoors or—when the weather is fine—grab a cone from the restaurant cart just outside and wend through the Village streets until the last drop is gone.   ALEX VAN BUREN

CAFÉ VIVA NATURAL PIZZA

Vegetarian, Pizzeria, Fast Food
2578 Broadway (97th & 98th St.)

212 663-8482
cafevivapizza.com
Daily: 11:30am–11:30pm

Those seeking more elbow room on the perennially crowded NYC subway should take the train uptown to Café Viva, where garlic—the infamous bulb credited with everything from warding off demons to curing toothaches over the course of history—is a major player. Tucked innocuously among Broadway's banks and bodegas, this vegetarian pizzeria offers more than this immune-system booster: All the cheese is kosher and hormone-free, and bread options include unbleached white flour, whole wheat, spelt and cornmeal. Some organic produce is available, as well, like that loaded onto a top-heavy Zen slice: shiitakes, sundried tomatoes, whole bulbs of garlic, fresh pesto and green tea-infused tofu. It sounds—and tastes—confusing, but it's not a bad option for vegans on the go.

And "on the go" is the way to dine here, instead of amid the bright burnt-orange walls and little red-and-chrome table sets. The spot is low on charm, but is a wise option for slice-cravers—especially since any sort of pie can be tailor-made. The pizza's good, though not award-winning, and includes a cheesy basic slice and an even better sauceless "Viva" on a whole-wheat crust topped with thin rounds of fresh tomatoes and nearly a handful of that fresh garlic. Skip pasta—noodles with a basic pomodoro were identical to what one can whip up at home—in favor of a side salad or a slice, and select an organic juice instead of sugary soda or ask for a glass of filtered water.

As for the garlic, it doesn't seem like owner Tony will be offering apologies for his addiction any time soon: He is so fond of the stuff that he commissioned a leggy cartoon bulb with his name on it to wave at you from behind the register while you buy your slice (wife Bella the Onion demurely bats her eyelashes). **ALEX VAN BUREN**

It's a good sign when you say to your waitress, "Do you have a favorite dessert?" and she replies instantly, with wide eyes, "Oh yes." Naturally sweetened desserts—delicious ones— have several hiding places in Gotham, and the Upper East Side's Candle Café is among the best: The chocolate mousse pie here would trick even a total sugar freak.

The Candle Café, the originator of nearby Candle 79, is old school. It's been a vegetarian hotspot for fifteen years. And even at 2:30 on a Wednesday afternoon, the 3rd Avenue location remains packed with locals. Minimalist black-and-tan chairs pushed next to square wooden tables make this a casual, take-your-mom-to-lunch-and-show-her-vegan-food-is-tasty sort of place.

CANDLE CAFÉ
Vegan
1307 Third Ave. (@75th St.)
212 472-0970
Mon–Sat: 11:30am–10:30pm,
Sun: 11:30am–9:30pm

CANDLE CAFÉ WEST
2427 Broadway
(89th & 90th St.)
212 769-8900
Mon-Sat: 11:30am–10:30pm,
Sun: 11:30am-9:30pm
candlecafe.com

Indeed, the menu ranges across the vegan landscape, with smoothies (we liked a Tropical Freeze packed with mango and pineapple), salads, sandwiches, and entrées— all of it organic. Those stopping in for a drink and a snack should indulge in a satisfyingly buttery-tasting tahini-based dip for focaccia, or a hearty, tasty "Aztec" salad draped with quinoa, topped with sticks of grilled tempeh and punched up with corn, beans, a mélange of greens and a brown, nutty sauce. The three-tiered "paradise casserole"—sweet potato, black beans and millet—was decent, with an earthy gravy and a pile of slightly bitter steamed bok choy, and my tofu BLT was just okay—but if nothing else, stop in post-shopping for a slice of that chocolate mousse pie or one of their seasonal (also sugar-free!) pies. The chocolate treat is absolutely decadent; tofu and coconut oil are whipped into a silky mousse that's decidedly un-tofulike, with a crumbly, chocolatey spelt crust that tastes nothing like spelt. The whole concoction is sweetened with maple syrup. Paired with a glass of organic Riesling after dinner, I was the happiest (healthy) sweets freak around.

ALEX VAN BUREN

CANDLE 79
Gourmet Vegan
154 E. 79th St.
(Lexington & 3rd Ave.) ④ ⑤ ⑥
212 537-7179
candle79.com
Mon–Sat: 12pm–3:30pm,
    5:30pm–10:30pm,
Sun: 12pm–4pm, 5pm–10pm

The posh elder sister of the chill Candle Café also offers a greatest-hits list of all-organic, vegan fare—tofu, tempeh, and falafel, oh, my!—to fussy Upper East Side denizens. Candle 79 is the fancier of the two, with a split-level, romantically lit interior full of plush, striped booths that encourage sprawling while dining. But stay upright long enough to select from the decent wine list, which features several biodynamic options, or tuck into luxuriously smooth guacamole, nicely showcasing the kitchen's skill with super-fresh produce or an addictive appetizer of long, rectangular blocks of lightly fried polenta. Move on to that ho-hum vegetarian standby, hummus, which gets a makeover here via red pepper-infused oil. A smoky bowl of it is served up with triangles of paratha bread, a full head of roasted garlic and a smattering of Kalamata olives. Similarly in the Mediterranean vein, a starter of hearts of palm salad mingles tiny shards of avocado with grape tomatoes and toasted pine nuts in an olive-balsamic vinaigrette. Entrées are simple but largely satisfying: Avoid the pitfalls of gluten-laden seitan in favor of, say, a cake made out of chickpeas, prettily presented, set in a drizzle of sweet coconut curry and wearing a hat of apricot chutney.

Unfortunately, the killer chocolate cake at Candle Café is not offered here, and the one naturally sweetened dessert we tried was just okay. If you must satiate that sweet tooth, housemade ginger ale—pristine leaves of mint floating in a tall glass swirling with fresh ginger, bubbly with soda water, and sweetened with agave— is excellent. It's touches like these that make this classy eatery quite popular with the UES set.

ALEX VAN BUREN

This assertively hippie-ish restaurant offers a kaleidoscopic array of vegan, kosher and raw foods to East Village locals and passersby. The space is long and slim, with low tin ceilings and petite tables swathed in printed, jewel-hued tablecloths. A long banquette leans up against the wall, enabling easy socializing. Though the space

CARAVAN OF DREAMS
Gourmet Vegan
405 E. 6th St. (1st Ave. & Ave. A)
④ ⑥ Ⓕ Ⓛ
212 254-1613
caravanofdreams.net
Mon-Fri: 11am-11pm,
Sat: 11am-12am,
Sun: 11am-11pm

is slightly below street level, large multi-paned windows near the front lend it an outdoorsy glow.

For the most part, the grub here is quite good, and smoothie-cravers should definitely put it on their map; we count a couple dozen fresh juices and shakes, along with booze like sangria (too tart on one visit) and several organic wines. Chill waiters seem unconcerned if you hang out for an hour or two over a beverage and a plate of "live" raw nachos: flaxseed chips with super-smooth guacamole, bright pico de gallo and almond sour cream (excellent on one visit, decent on another). We loved a Mexican-themed platter stacked with slices of toothsome grilled tempeh, tender black beans and sweet grilled bananas on a pile of mixed veggies. On the health front, the eatery wins points for abundant organic options, more than a dozen salads on offer, the fact that sandwiches are available on sprouted whole-grain bread, and wheat-free choices like a fluffy spelt pancake served with a tiny pitcher of top-notch maple syrup. Though we weren't wowed by the naturally sweetened desserts we tried, we'll come back to keep noshing through the epic menu because the Caravan has ambiance in spades: A single mother sat down beside us, and by meal's end we knew her baby's name (Leo), her homeland (Germany), and her baby's weight (9 lbs; we ended up holding him so she could finish her meal). Some restaurants are unconcerned about looking hippie-ish, and Caravan of Dreams, happily, is one of them.

ALEX VAN BUREN

CHIPOTLE
Mexican, Fast Food
Multiple Locations (see website)
chipotle.com

Ah, Chipotle: The burrito chain we need not feel guilty about loving. Though recent years bore witness to a wave of panic among Chipotle-lovers, as women and men across the city panicked upon learning that their lunchtime burrito could run them up to 1,000 calories, this chain (there are lots citywide) counts us among its fans. If you wish, tailor your burrito or "burrito bol" (Jared recommends getting bol or a salad) to be less heavy—drop the sour cream, ask for a mere sprinkling of cheese, or save half a portion for later—and rejoice in the all antibiotic-free meat, the organic cheese and the downright tasty grub. All the meats are great, particularly spicy, cumin scented *barbacoa* (beef) and tender pulled *al pastor* (pork). Indeed, even local superstar chef David Chang of pig-obsessed mini-chain Momofuku tried to get a job at Chipotle in order to find out how they make their pork, but was rejected. "They knew what I was up to," he said sadly. So swing by with fellow meat-lovers or even vegetarians: Though options are a bit more sparse for the latter, the veggie burrito bol can be strewn with green peppers and onions, black beans (caveat: the pinto beans are mixed with decidedly un-vegetarian bacon) and all sorts of fresh salsas and guacamole. The guacamole here is quite good; if you want a little more kick to yours, just spritz it with one of the free fresh lime wedges by the napkin stash. There are few fast-food chains at which to get a surprisingly healthy fix in the city, and even fewer that taste this good.

ALEX VAN BUREN

Ciao for Now is the epitome of sustainable. They use local vendors for almost everything, from coffee to grass-fed beef to nitrate-free bacon. They have an electric car for deliveries, they compost all food waste, and they use quadruple-filtered water for all of their cooking, baking, and beverage making.

The space is bright and beautiful with large windows, mismatched tables and service stations, stools and benches. The staff is genuine and sweet as they offer their recommendations: "We have two soups, but you want the red lentil with coconut milk." (They were right—it was delicious.)

CIAO FOR NOW
New American, Bakery
523 E 12th St. (Ave. A & Ave. B) Ⓛ
212 677-2616
Mon–Fri: 7:30am–6pm,
Sat: 8am–5pm,
Sun: 8:30am–5pm

107 W. 10th St. (@ 6th Ave.)
Ⓑ Ⓓ Ⓕ Ⓜ Ⓛ ① ② ③
212 929-8363
Mon–Fri: 8am–6pm,
Sat–Sun: 9am–5pm
ciaofornow.net

Unlike the stellar service, unfortunately, the food can be hit or miss. The roasted beet salad with its familiar companions of pecan and fresh goat cheese was large and delicious, and the chili-oil vegetable stir-fry with quinoa was really good and tasted more grilled than stir-fried. The turkey sandwich was fine, on nicely textured nine-grain bread, but the turkey, while free-range, tasted like it was sliced more than a couple of hours before we ate it. Ciao for Now also does brunch, and while the menu items look interesting (savory French toast with red onion confit), some fall flat. The huevos verdes were strange, overcooked and covered a ragout of tasty vegetables and pieces of tortilla that had dissolved into a corny mush that was less than desirable.

However, we're willing to forgive occasional missteps, and Ciao for Now redeems itself with an array of pastries and breakfast items including tasty vegan banana muffins and a fair selection of naturally sweetened desserts (featuring a chocolate espresso cookie and snack bar sweetened with agave and dried fruits). As an added bonus, the prices are as friendly as the staff, so you can afford to test out both locations.

TALIA BERMAN

CITRUS GRILL
Latin, Asian
320 Amsterdam Ave. (@ 75th St.)
① ② ③ Ⓑ Ⓒ
212 595-0500
citrusnyc.com
Mon–Thu: 5:30pm–11pm,
Fri: 5:30pm–12am,
Sat: 11:30am–3:45pm, 5pm–12am,
Sun: 11:30am–11pm

Like its sister restaurant the neighborhood-y Josie's, Citrus Bar & Grill has its own identity: Trend Central. Oddly enough for a spot on the Upper West Side, it is vaguely reminiscent of South Beach, with a spacey bright orange and white palette and silver-rimmed stools lining the bar.

Like its menu, the eatery is split as though by a knife down its middle. The lower level is all sleek banquettes and bright colors, whereas the second level boasts minimalist decor and a sushi bar home to stern looking chefs. This is not a subtle distinction, and the website drives it home further: "Latin Fare, Asian Flair." Okay, we get it! Sometimes the schtick works beautifully, as in a trio of tacos: toothsome Brandt beef drizzled with tomatillo salsa, a classic pork-and-pineapple combo and chicken with a mango sauce served with mixed greens drizzled with a sprightly miso-carrot dressing. Sometimes it doesn't, as in an ill-advised appetizer of edamame topped with overly-smoky ancho chile powder. Entrées are decent here, and include a plate of tender Long Island duck breast with a side of savory mashed sweet potatoes and haricot verts. A side of kale, meanwhile, was over-sautéed and a bit too garlicky (hopefully an anomaly).

So nosh along the menu—it's certainly epic. And don't forget to sample the fruits of the sea: Silky wild salmon on brown rice was very good, and clearly fresh. Since so much of the fare served at Louis Lanza's empire is organic, it's best to head here for a clever mix of cuisines, and to Josie's for all-organic produce.   ALEX VAN BUREN

Many of us are lured through the inviting doors of City Bakery and—not seeing the forest for the trees—halt like five-year-olds in front of the aromatic, bubbling hot chocolate machines. Though the Union Square shop's cocoa is famous for a reason, be sure to sample the often-excellent, always local and mostly organic savory fare. Not only will this cut that hit of sugar to the old bloodstream, but eco-friendly paper boxes can be filled with a myriad of savory eats to hustle over to one of several tiny, round tables in the split-level space. Hot and cold buffets feature fare that utterly defeats salad-bar stereotypes, including sprightly cilantro-flecked grilled chicken and dreamily tender roast sweet potatoes studded with golden pineapple cubes. Even soups and stews are a success, including a ratatouille so richly aromatic it would cut through a head cold. Several salads are always on offer, and I couldn't get enough of a lentil number—and I am no lentil proponent, I assure you—proving that the Bakery does well by tough-to-love items, too. (Listen up, people with kids!) So if you need to trick little Jimmy into some greens alongside his cocoa, this might just be the place to do it.

Those stopping in for brunch will be just as pleased; organic eggs come strewn with red pepper and shards of green onion, and an excellent French toast is crackly like a crème brûlée and served alongside organic, top-grade maple syrup. This is part of many foodie tours of the city, and popular with locals—witness the cute couples huddling over those tiny tables, and the women meeting for a chat—though the hubbub downstairs can be deafening weekends and weeknights, so plan your visit carefully.   ALEX VAN BUREN

CITY BAKERY
American, Juice Bar
3 W. 18th St. (5th & 6th Ave.)
①②③④⑤⑥ⓃⓆⓇⒻⓂⓁ
212 366-1414
thecitybakery.com
Mon–Fri: 7:30am–7pm,
Sat: 8am–7pm,
Sun: 10am–6pm

COLICCHIO AND SONS

New American

85 Tenth Ave. (@ 15th st.)  Ⓐ Ⓒ Ⓔ Ⓛ

212 400-6699

colicchioandsons.com

Mon–Thu: 12pm–2:30pm,
    6pm–10pm,
Fri: 12pm–2:30pm, 5:30pm–11pm,
Sat: 11am–2:30pm, 5pm–11pm,
Sun: 11am–2:30pm, 5pm–9pm

The newest member of celebrity chef Tom Colicchio's Manhattan restaurant empire, the gleaming and opulent Colicchio and Sons, sits on a far-flung stretch of 10th Ave. Oddly situated on a desolate street corner across from a gas station, Colicchio and Sons is really just Chef Colicchio's reinvention of Craftsteak, a high-end black leather-coated steakhouse. The beauty of the space hasn't changed much (and neither has the slinky service) but the concept has—a little more local, a tad more focused, and when he's not shilling Diet Coke or critiquing Top Chefs, Colicchio is actually chef whites and all, manning the kitchen.

Colicchio's laudable track record steepened our expectations; however, on last visit we were a bit disappointed by some lackluster menu options. A root vegetable salad went raw rather than roasted which made for a clean and refreshing dish but needed a tad more dressing. A duck breast with farro was cooked perfectly but lacked the spice the menu proclaimed.

There were highlights though: small squid stuffed with Tuscan kale over a sultry black-ink risotto and venison with huckleberry sauce and celery root gratin were pitch-perfect. In accordance with the market-driven movement, the menu changes often, so there are always gems to be discovered.

Happily, some things have remained constant: the vegetables and protein are carefully sourced from smaller farms that Colicchio has been working with for years, and the menu, which leans on Spanish and Indian flavors, remains rooted in fine French technique and American comfort. Nibbling local turnips under a glass fortress of the finest vintages at Colicchio and Sons while watching the Top Chef at work is an easy way to celebrate both locavorism and fine dining.   SCARLETT LINDEMAN

That the proprietors of longtime downtown fave Clinton Street Baking Company are still succeeding at comfort fare—now across town, in Morningside Heights—will come as no surprise to those who wait in long lines for their burgers and brunch. Happily, the eatery has not only a different menu, but a greater focus on organic fare. We snagged seats on the sidewalk under the luminous, gawk-worthy lanterns, but suspect

COMMUNITY FOOD AND JUICE
New American

2893 Broadway (112th & 113th St.)
212 665-2800
communityrestaurant.com
Mon-Thu: 8am-3:30pm, 5pm-9:30pm,
Fri: 8am-3:30pm, 5pm-10pm,
Sat: 9am-3:30pm, 5pm-10pm,
Sun: 9am-3:30pm, 5pm-9:30pm

we would have been just as happy inside, esconced on a long banquette facing the slim, industrial space. Tall ceilings and floor-to-ceiling windows do a fine job letting the light shine in, and exposed piping gives an aura of an art gallery-cum-eatery.

Health-friendly options abound, starting with the beverages: Water is filtered, and there are a dozen organic or sustainable vino options for those who tipple. And vegetables prance happily across the menu, from a local tomato salad dotted with homemade ricotta to a jewel-hued, tender "bowl of beets" married to sweet goat cheese, to the substantial, choose-your-own-veggie sides alongside the fish and meat of the day. Of these, you'll have to pick and choose to find the best: We weren't thrilled by undercooked brussels sprouts that came alongside a juicy organic strip steak topped with a melting slab of herb-spiked butter. The fish of the day did better, arriving plump and tender atop a tumble of sautéed onions and mushrooms in a pool of Thai red curry sauce to swipe them through. Among ample vegetarian options are the rice bowl—a simple mix of brown rice, prettily julienned carrots and cukes, bean sprouts and bright bits of cilantro and mint, with a sesame-lime dressing to tie the whole together. Mercifully, you can even end this meal feeling good: The eatery is certified by the Green Restaurant Association for its environmentally sound practices, from composting to energy-efficient kitchen equipment. ALEX VAN BUREN

COOKSHOP
New American
156 10th Ave. @ 20th St. Ⓐ Ⓒ Ⓔ
212 924-4440
cookshopny.com
Mon–Fri: 8am–11am, 11:30am–4pm,
    5:30pm–11:30pm,
Sat–Sun: 10:30am–4pm,
    5:30pm–11:30pm

Looking at art while gallivanting around Chelsea is hunger-inducing, so thank goodness for places like Cookshop, where the fabulous people brunch. Every table in the clean, high-ceilinged eatery—it resembles a gallery in layout—seemed to be occupied with a moneyed arty type or L.A. transplant. In short, this is where Chelsea denizens (and their friends) brunch. Occasional tourists seem to be acceptable, as long as they look good.

The fare was solid, with a few standouts: Though we were disappointed by the refined sugar on the table and the fact that not all produce was organic, husband-wife owner team Vicki Freeman and Marc Meyer (see Hundred Acres and Five Points) pride themselves on sourcing locally, and it shows. For one, a giant chalkboard in the back of the restaurant features a diagram of a cow's edible parts—thank goodness the chef does well by the mooing stuff. The tender beef brisket we dove into was carved from cows raised on an eco-friendly farm in Virginia: Bits of sweet caramelized onions floated alongside punchy bits of red pepper, with the whites of two perfectly poached eggs making a ghostly trail atop the whole. Less impressive was the buzzed-about Cookshop Scramble: Though it's worth sampling for those organic eggs, the taste of applewood bacon was muted, as was the crème fraîche supposedly mixed in. Opt, instead, for antibiotic-free chicken salad. Thick slabs of the bird come on a giant pile of mixed greens spruced up with green olives, golden raisins and a splash of tart, Mediterranean-inspired vinaigrette. Sea salt is on every table, we noted, so one can sprinkle a few crystals on anything lacking. Happily, at Cookshop, not much is, including the people-watching. As we left, a woman preened on the outdoor patio, sunning herself in a hat that looked to have been vertically sliced in half—an ode to Picasso, perhaps? Ah, Chelsea.

ALEX VAN BUREN

Tom Colicchio evidently heeds his own recycled Top Chef advice—that cooking simple food with quality ingredients will yield the most successful results—at this arm of his prosperous Craft restaurant empire. Sharing is encouraged in the long, terracotta-colored dining room—the menu options are separated into first and main course sections, then further divided into protein, vegetable, and cooking method subcategories. Those who dislike surprises will rejoice as dishes arrive exactly as they are described in the organized menu.

CRAFT
New American
43 E. 19th St. (Broadway &
Park Ave South)
④ ⑤ ⑥ Ⓝ Ⓡ Ⓠ Ⓛ
212 780-0880
craftrestaurant.com
Sun–Th: 5:30pm–10:00pm,
Fri–Sat: 5:30pm–11:00pm

That is not to say, however, that any one selection will be uninteresting — corn and bacon risotto, rightfully recommended by our waiter, employed its promised crisp, salty bacon and succulent corn pieces in a concoction that was unexpectedly creamy and addicting. The other rich dish we ordered, the zucchini agnolotti, incorporates a tangy, pinkish sauce atop generously stuffed pockets. Despite its inclusion of cream, this small plate remains refreshingly light. Hen of the woods mushrooms self-assuredly approach the table as is with need no additional enhancement. They're seasoned enough to justify the absence of a saltshaker without disguising their naturally earthy taste. All of Craft's meats are local, sustainable, and superbly cooked — quail is lightly charred and flavorful, and braised short rib absorbs its thick, sticky gravy. Chicken, moist on the inside and topped with a rosemary sprig, comes fresh from the oven in its own brassy saucepan. Lucky for diners, the phrase "do as I say, not as I do" is a moot point when it comes to Tom Colicchio's culinary skills. He competently cooks clean, New American food without unnecessarily over-thinking his menu.

ALLIX GENESLAW

DEL POSTO

Italian
85 Tenth Ave. (@ 16th St.)
① ② ③ Ⓐ Ⓒ Ⓔ Ⓛ
212 497-8090
delposto.com
Mon–Fri: 11:30am–2pm,
    5:30pm–11pm,
Sat: 4:30pm–11pm,
Sun: 4:30pm–10pm

The stretch of 10th Avenue between 15th and 16th Streets is home to two culinary landmarks as hulking and formidable as their celebrity chef owners—the neighboring Colicchio & Sons (formerly Craftsteak of Tom Colicchio's empire) and Del Posto (owned in part by Mario Batali). Other than a ho-hum view of the Garden State and the nearby Chelsea Market, the exclusive tinted windows and attention-commanding heft of these two giants lend bragging rights to this fairly industrial part of town.

Del Posto's breathtaking interior supplants diners in a setting comparable to that of a luxury hotel lobby; the reception podium is recessed, allowing each guest to make a majestic entrance via split marble staircases. A longer, wider staircase leads to more private balcony seating along the perimeter, while the first floor is divided into two roomy sections with chestnut leather booths and free-standing tables.

At times, the hospitality sentiment progresses past the initial aesthetic and becomes a comically oppressive production during the meal. Servers precisely synchronize their delivery of dishes, dropping exotic insalata primavera, cotechino with spiced fruit and lentils, and coarsely chopped carne cruda starters onto the table in unison. Second courses are protein-heavy but also come with their fair share of vegetable sides. Both duck and lamb boast ruddy complexions and impossibly tender meat. The former is complemented by endive and apricots; the latter is enhanced by a cool, pucker-inducing yogurt and Swiss chard ragu. A barely pink pork slab is served with peas, multicolored string beans, and succulent cannellini beans.

Del Posto's delicious, plentiful food, soothing piano tunes, and exceptional service are certainly worth a visit.   ALLIX GENESLAW

Founder Adam Eskin has revamped his body-building-protein-shake-90's-approach of The Pump to focus on quality sourcing, seasonal ingredients and excellent taste at Dig Inn. At lunch, an s-shaped queue moved quickly as we gawked at the menu. Diners create small or large market plates from the flavorful selection of Chef Daniel Angerer's hormone- and antibiotic-free proteins, vegetables, grains, and sauces.

DIG INN SEASONAL MARKET
American, Fast Food, Juice Bar
Multiple Locations (see website)
diginn.com

Jared's favorite was the all-natural shredded Pineland beef shoulder, braised to perfection in oregano and an appealingly astringent red wine vinegar. Conversely, chicken with subtle touches of paprika and lime was versatile and brightened a bland side of cauliflower with chickpeas. The roasted sweet potato side, with hints of paprika, rosemary, and earthy mushrooms with chopped celery, was reminiscent of stuffing.

Seasonal specials were standouts, particularly a mayo-free wild salmon salad with moist, miso-marinated salmon, diced cucumbers, and sweet red bell peppers in a light, tart red wine vinaigrette. A tangy carrot-ginger dressing and shaved green apples finished surprisingly tender and flavor-packed local kale.

Raw, cold-pressed juices, smoothies and shakes are made to order with chia seed, flax seed, SunWarrior vegan protein or soy milk enhancements. Ginger fanatics may enjoy the spicy Pomegranate Pear, a blend of bartlett pears, ginger, mint, pomegranate juice and agave, but the gritty texture wasn't our favorite. Next time, we'd stick with the pineapple coconut smoothie with extra basil—but hold the agave to avoid the cloying sweetness.

Dig Inn's customizable menu offers carnivores options while vegetarians can fill up on organic tofu and protein-rich quinoa, and everyone can benefit from a veggie overload with the sides. With locations throughout the city, delivery available and economic prices, Dig Inn gives every New Yorker access to a healthy and satisfying meal.

CHELSEA GRANT

DIRTY BIRD TO-GO

American, Fast Food
204 W. 14th St. (7th & 8th Ave.)
① ② ③ Ⓐ Ⓒ Ⓔ Ⓕ Ⓜ Ⓛ PATH
212 620-4836
Mon–Fri: 11am–11pm,
Sat–Sun: 11:30am–11pm

155 Chambers St. (@ W. Broadway)
① ② ③ ④ ⑤ ⑥ Ⓐ Ⓒ Ⓔ Ⓝ Ⓡ Ⓙ Ⓩ
212 964-3284
dirtybirdtogo.com
Mon–Fri: 10:30am–10pm,
Sat–Sun: 11:30am–10pm

Only in New York can you snag an order "to go" from a tiny, nondescript fried chicken joint and realize—probably after sinking your teeth into a crisp-skinned, slow-roasted rotisserie bird or an astoundingly juicy fried drumstick—that this is grub from a haute cuisine veteran and a James Beard Award (the Oscars of food) winner. Former Dirty Bird owner and recipe developer Allison Vines-Rushing has worked with renowned international restaurateur Alain Ducasse, and although you

wouldn't think a simple bite of bird would reveal her vast skills, you'd be wrong.

The fare Dirty Bird is turning out in a tiny to-go spot just north of the West Village is, believe it or not, good for you. Of course, rotisserie chicken is a healthier choice than the crispy stuff (which is soaked in buttermilk and fried in peanut oil), but every Dirty Bird sent out the door is hormone- and antibiotic-free and locally raised. And if you have to go for the fried stuff, the oil they use for frying is recycled for biodiesel fuel. Sin with a side of sautéed garlic kale—it's excellent here, locally grown and dotted with chili peppers and garlic—instead of the few drab iceberg salad numbers. Take note: The joint means it when it calls itself "to-go"; seats are few and far between. But swing by with a friend who doesn't mind the hubbub of a largely takeout operation, and enjoy the not-at-all-dirty birds.　　　ALEX VAN BUREN

Elizabeth's Neighborhood Table adds some suburban flair to the Upper West Side with a lemony exterior and picturesque white picket fence. Inside, a restaurant and bar with a casual American feel serves up thoughtful comfort food.

ELIZABETH'S NEIGHBORHOOD TABLE
American
680 Columbus Ave. (W. 93rd & W. 94th St)
① ② ③ Ⓑ Ⓒ
212 280-6500
elizabethsnyc.com
Mon–Fri: 11:30am–3:30pm,
    5:30pm–10:30pm,
Sat–Sun: 11am–3:30pm, 5:30pm–10:30pm

A hearty appetizer selection included grass-fed beef sliders, chicken wings and steamed mussels. We ordered the jumbo lump Maryland crab cakes and the vegetable tempura. Two perfectly crisp crab cakes drizzled with a creamy homemade white sauce topped a mound of shaved apple and fennel. The tempura breading was light (but still fairly greasy) and encased fresh market vegetables like fennel, yellow squash and broccoli. A tangy curry-yogurt dipping sauce was a welcome change from the traditional soy.

A simple mesclun mix from North Fork's Satur Farm formed the house salad. Very lightly dressed with sherry-lime vinaigrette, the salad included slices of radish and long thin ribbons of carrots, which added a splash of color. The homemade veggie burger arrived with avocado and sunflower sprouts, all served on a hearty wheat toast with a side of salad. The incredibly satisfying veggie patty was full of grains and vegetables like onions and shredded carrots, and we were happy to find organic ketchup available. When it came to the grass-fed angus steak, we wished the entire steak was edible and consistently cooked throughout. There was quite a bit of fat and cartilage that could have been trimmed off, but when we were able to get a bite of beef, it was succulent.

Large portions and the casual restaurant decor may call to mind a chain eatery, but at Elizabeth's, meats are all local and hormone- and antibiotic free, beef is grass-fed, salmon is sustainable, the produce is often organic, and the dishes are satisfying.   AMY SUNG

ELLARY'S GREENS

New American, Juice Bar

33 Carmine St. (Bleecker St. & Bedford St.) ① Ⓐ Ⓑ Ⓒ Ⓓ Ⓔ Ⓕ Ⓜ

212 920-5072

www.ellarysgreens.com

Mon–Fri: 7am–11pm,
Sat: 10am–11pm,
Sun: 10am–10pm

Tucked away on Carmine Street, Ellary's Greens is bringing healthy and affordable gourmet dining to the West Village. The ingredients used in this contemporary café are local, organic, and/or natural, with an emphasis on high quality and nutrition. The stylish interior showcases a casual vibe with exposed brick walls, green-leaf ceiling décor, recessed lighting, and tufted banquettes.

The expansive menu employs symbols to denote vegan, vegetarian, dairy-free, and gluten-free items. Start with one of the daily soup selections or fresh salads, like our pick of nori seaweed with sliced cucumber, daikon and napa cabbage dressed with a citrus vinaigrette. Other light fare includes paninis and sandwiches, including a BLT (with house-cured, smoked bacon) and a crumbly manchego cheese layered with chestnut purée, orange marmalade and frisée on whole wheat bread.

Protein entrées, vegetable dishes, and seasonal sides round out the savory offerings. Our grilled salmon filet arrived nicely cooked but was overpowered by a too-tart lemon confit emulsion. However, we were delighted by the green thai curry: the flavorful, spice-hinted sauce coating a bowl of tofu, tender sweet potatoes and green beans was exceptional. Vietnamese brown rice noodles tossed with halved poached shrimp and egg ribbons in garlicky Nuoc Cham sauce was a refreshing gluten-free pasta alternative, and the Lebanese-style quinoa-stuffed zucchini rounds over tomato-yogurt purée proved a flavorsome accompaniment.

Refreshments range from cold-pressed juices and Brooklyn-brewed kombucha to biodynamic wine and gluten-free beers. Early risers can wake up to Ellary's weekday breakfast with cage-free eggs and tofu scrambles, house-made biscuits and almond pancakes with blueberries and coconut cream. Try to snag a sidewalk seat during warmer months or settle into a sun-drenched table by the windows for a naturally delicious experience.   MEGAN MURPHY

In NYC Italian cuisine runs the gamut from take-out slices to coveted dining at celebrity chef-owned upscale restaurants. Somewhere in between we find Emporio—the sister location of Aurora Soho and Brooklyn—a vintage-outfitted downtown pizza emporium boasting a wine bar, open kitchen and light-filled atrium dining room.

EMPORIO
Italian
231 Mott St. (Prince St. & Spring St.)
⑥ Ⓑ Ⓓ Ⓕ Ⓙ Ⓜ Ⓩ Ⓝ Ⓡ
212 966-1234
emporiony.com
Mon–Wed: 11am–11pm,
Thu–Sat: 11am–12am,
Sun: 11am–10:30pm

Farm fresh salads highlight the season's produce as yellow and green heirloom string beans are tossed into an insalate with shaved pecorino while peaches are balanced with peppery arugula, toasted hazelnuts and one of Italy's most popular cheeses, Grana Padano DOP.

Emporio sources from local farmer's markets as much as possible; this is clear when you bite into the delicately crafted oversized raviolis stuffed with buffalo mozzarella and black olives. The final addition of colorful chunks of heirloom tomatoes and baby zucchini made this pasta dish perfectly succulent. We were happy to see that gluten-free renditions of the pastas and pizzas are also on offer. We tried one of these gluten-free pizzas, an artichoke, mushroom, ham, and San Marzano tomato creation dolloped with fior di latte mozzarella, but our choice to order it without the ham resulted in an under seasoned pizza. Perhaps we should have trusted the chef's preparation; we certainly enjoyed the thin, crunchy, cracker-like crust.

The secondi are where Emporio really shines. Conscious eaters will be happy that the meats and fish are sustainably sourced while foodies will relish the perfectly balanced preparations. The grass-fed NY strip from Painted Hill Farm is delightfully tender, juicy, and complemented with roasted cipollini onions, rosemary potatoes and a tasty salsa verde. The chicken under a brick is free-range and perfectly complemented with cranberry beans, broccoli raab, and applewood-smoked bacon. The excellent food and responsible sourcing are sure to have me coming back to Emporio to satisfy my Italian cravings.   LISA LEEKING RUVALCABA

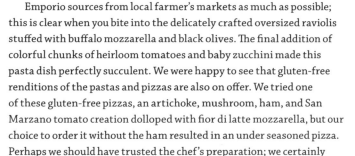

115

THE FAT RADISH

New American, British
17 Orchard St.
(Canal & Hester St.)

Ⓑ Ⓓ Ⓕ Ⓙ Ⓜ Ⓩ

212 300-4053
thefatradishnyc.com
Mon–Fri: 12pm–3:30pm, 5:30pm–12am,
Sat: 11am–3:30pm, 5:30pm–12am,
Sun: 11am–3:30pm, 5:30pm–10pm

The phrase "farm-to-table" has become a favorite of many New York restaurants, so much so that you might understandably be skeptical of its authenticity. The Fat Radish, however, is the real deal. British chef-owner Ben Towill is as adept at coaxing bold flavors from humble vegetables as he is fastidious about where he sources from—places like Brooklyn's Pierless Fish and Garden of Spices poultry farm in upstate New York.

A plate of heirloom carrots arrived integrity-intact, satisfyingly firm beside a tussle of crispy and sautéed kale, with bits of hijiki seaweed emitting miso-scented steam. The Market Salad of seven different greens was a study in freshness, a marriage of buttery and bitter flavors enhanced with subtle lemon vinaigrette and ricotta salata. Towill and fellow Brit co-owner Phil Winser also lead a sustainable catering and lifestyle company called Silkstone, which designed the interior of the East Village eatery—a space so soothing in its industrial-meets-organic aesthetic that it borders on precious. The menu's pungent originality nicely balances all the worn wood and weathered white brick, lit by candles and scented with potted herbs. Red cabbage slaw had kick and bite, a spicy counterpoint to sweet rutabaga smash and a juicy Heritage Farm pork chop. Likewise, pan-seared striped bass arrived perfectly cooked and snowy white beside sweet roasted radishes and turnips, sliced thinly and glazed with miso. Rarely does minimalism convey such depth—proteins betray no seasoning but taste and feel satisfying, especially when sprinkled with sea salt from the little bowls atop each table. Duck rillette terrine, made in-house, was gently gamey and as appealing solo as it was atop toast slathered with grainy mustard and mellow onion jam. Ingredients like these, capable of standing alone as well as they combine, are precisely why the farm-to-table movement perpetuates.   SARAH AMANDOLARE

This flagship of the Marc Meyer/ Vicki Freeman triumvirate (Hundred Acres, Cookshop) was established in 1999 and remains a champion of locally procured goods and organic animal products. The pan-American eatery is more sizable than its sisters: To walk in is to immediately note its high ceilings and long bar teeming with patrons clamoring for a glass of wine or a unique cocktail (lime-

FIVE POINTS
New American
31 Great Jones St. (Lafayette St. & Bowery) ⑥ Ⓑ Ⓓ Ⓕ Ⓜ Ⓝ Ⓡ
212 253-5700
fivepointsrestaurant.com
Mon–Fri: 12pm–11pm,
Sat: 10:30am–3pm, 5:30pm–11pm,
Sun: 10:30am–3pm, 5:30pm–10pm

and-lavender gimlet, anyone?). Keep going and take a gander at that "fountain" slimly lining the room; it's a hollowed-out oak tree.

The fare here is likewise solid and hearty—bistro food with a kick. Line-caught Alaskan salmon may not be regional (it is FedExed in each morning), but it was perhaps the best we sampled. The flesh was rosy and luscious, and served atop a summery ragout of pigeon peas, green beans, corn and sparkly mint. We couldn't get enough of it. Pair it with a starter of wild arugula and goat cheese salad dressed with a simple roast shallot and olive oil vinaigrette—we dropped our forks swearing we'd not eat anything else for the duration of the summer. Carnivores can tuck into a grass-fed burger topped with fat, lazy slabs of smoked bacon, so juicy it required extra napkins. The sole disappointment was pasta: An entrée portion of house-made cavatelli mingling with bacon, roast corn and chives lacked kick. But this airy, elegant space deserves another visit; the service was smart, adeptly pairing a not-too-sweet Riesling with our salmon. (Though there were no organic or local vinos by the glass, draft beers included local suds-makers Sixpoint and Captain Lawrence.) Next time we might reserve the large, pretty table lit by a skylight in the back of the restaurant—ideal for a celebratory dinner out.   ALEX VAN BUREN

FREEFOODS
American
18 W. 45th St. (5th & 6th Ave.)
①②③Ⓢ④⑤⑥⑦ⓃⓆⓇ
ⒶⒸⒺⒷⒹⒻⓂ
212 302-7195
freefoodsnyc.com
Mon–Fri: 8am–8pm

"Eat. Think. Be Organic," read the brown t-shirts of the workers at this Rockefeller Center area lunch spot. Indeed, it's a clean place to eat clean food, and perhaps the brightest with natural light of any we surveyed. Floor-to-ceiling windows illuminate comfy, Jetsons-like brown-and-white swivel stools at the eatery, which features an impressive salad bar, a number of raw foods, and many vegetarian and vegan items.

Matthew Kenney, an original owner of Pure Food and Wine, is the man behind the eats here—soups, salads and hot entrées—and although it costs a couple dollars more than at nearby eateries, all the grub is organic, and yes, you can taste it. Both soups we tried—a decadent lobster bisque and a vegan soup that somehow mustered a creamy zucchini/ split-pea base that was not too "vegetable-y"—impressed us, as did a made-to-order salad with a tangy gingery dressing, crunchy chickpeas and sprightly baby arugula. Pre-prepared offerings varied a little more in quality: Salmon flecked with mango was a touch overcooked, and a terrine of tomato sauce, raw tomatoes, pesto and nut cheese was just...so...tomato-y. Nor did I love our bland tofu sandwich. That said, a charming level of eavesdropping is the name of the game here, and long raised shared tables almost seem to encourage flirting among the cleancut midtown types. Jared was pleased to see a few vegan desserts, including a few containing organic sugar, though he would have preferred to see agave used. Most important, FreeFoods takes its nature schtick seriously. Not only do blades of grass and bright blue skies line the posted menus, but all cutlery and cupware is biodegradable.

ALEX VAN BUREN

Rarely does the philosophy of economics make its way into a restaurant—but then again, Friedman's Lunch isn't your average restaurant. Named after economist Milton Friedman (who famously said, "There's no such thing as a free lunch"), this Chelsea Market restaurant strives to provide an atmosphere Mr. Friedman would approve: delicious and healthy food served at reasonable prices.

FRIEDMAN'S LUNCH
American
75 9th Ave. (15th & 16th St.)
Ⓐ Ⓒ Ⓔ Ⓛ ① ②
212 929-7100
friedmanslunch.com
Mon–Fri: 8am–9pm,
Sat: 10am–9pm,
Sun: 10am–8pm

Beyond the warm wood floors and black chalkboards (noting a fresh-squeezed fruit juice of the day), I happily noted an open kitchen and a chef holding a beautiful fresh bundle of kale. Our knowledgeable server steered us away from non-organic items (fish tacos with citrus-fennel slaw and sriracha aioli sounded tempting, but corn tortillas weren't organic and non-GMO). My curiosity got the best of me so I began with the kale salad with tangy pink grapefruit, shaved red onion, and citronette. Other satisfying salad options include a seared fillet of salmon served over crunchy romaine hearts with crisp cucumber, shaved carrots, crumbly feta cheese, and a creamy dill dressing.

As the entrees arrived, seemingly standard dishes surprised with deeply developed flavor profiles. The brown rice bowl—a sometimes undeniably boring dish—was elevated by meaty Japanese eggplant and a hint of smoke from sesame oil. Bok choy, edamame, carrots, and bean sprouts complete this nutrient-packed entree (available with grilled chicken or tofu). If you're craving a burger and fries, hope that Chelsea Market is within striking distance. The Creekstone Farms ground brisket burger was nourishing and tender, and herbed fries sent the aroma of rosemary wafting around the table. While servers could have kept a closer eye on our water glasses, their friendly nature also contributes to the relaxed ambiance. Even Milton Friedman would agree that when it comes to good value, this restaurant provides guilt-free temptation.

JESSICA COLLEY

GOBO
Gourmet Vegetarian
401 6th Ave. (Waverly Pl. & 8th St.)
① Ⓐ Ⓒ Ⓔ Ⓑ Ⓓ Ⓕ Ⓜ
212 255-3902
Daily: 11:30am-10:30pm

1426 3rd Ave. (@ 81st St.) ④ ⑤ ⑥
212 288-4686
Daily: 12pm-10:30pm
goborestaurant.com

As the heavy, forbidding wooden doors that grace its entryway suggest, this eatery offers Serious Vegetarian Fare. Even the notoriously veggie-blind food press has paid the restaurant (and its uptown sibling) notice, with a review in the "\$25 and Under" section of *The New York Times*. Gobo's atmosphere is reminiscent of an upscale sushi restaurant embedded in a posh salon: Cushioned banquettes line the walls and three elegant, boxy

lighting fixtures illuminate the stretch of the main hallway. At night, the joint is jumping, but at lunchtime your companions might include only a few quiet businessmen sipping sweet pineapple iced teas. And although service was a little scattered, our dishes came flying out of the kitchen.

We'd have to agree with the paper of record's assessment that the fare is a bit hit-or-miss. But when it hits, it hits hard. Pick among the menu and be sure to avoid the processed soy products—they're everywhere, and they're not good for you—and instead select a tasty starter like lightly fried scallion pancakes topped with a pyramid of sweet mango salsa or a packed-with-minerals seaweed, kale and beet salad. Soups seem to be among the kitchen's forte; a calming, wintry number came with a broth so savory it resembled chicken broth, with a few root vegetables and tender white beans lazing about. Of the entrées, try an autumnal faux-lasagna—sweet potatoes layered with rice "pasta" and kale was a quite convincing incarnation of the classic, though it might not fool your Italian cousin—rather than a gummy green beans-and-eggplant creation, which had been over-sautéed. Though no desserts are sugar-free, a vast selection of fruit-packed, sugar-free smoothies are available, and tipplers can peruse an impressive list of wine and beers that include several organics, putting the cap on the notion that this is fine vegetarian dining, indeed.   ALEX VAN BUREN

This member of Danny Meyer's coterie (including Tabla and Eleven Madison Park) occupies a sedate stretch just north of shopper-packed Union Square. The eatery has received renewed attention since chef Michael Anthony took the helm in 2007, and with a focus on knowing its farmers, ensuring sustainable use of animals, and local, mostly organic produce, it deserves it.

Two restaurants essentially cohabit one awning: Up front is a casual tavern featuring broad, blowsy murals of cabbages and onions, and a long, wooden bar. Profusions of flowers in the foyer call to mind an elegant potpourri shop, and the more formal dining room features Impressionist-era portraits, so this is definitely where we'll bring Mom when she's in town.

GRAMERCY TAVERN

New American

42 E 20th St. (Park Ave. South & Broadway) ④ ⑤ ⑥ Ⓝ Ⓠ Ⓡ Ⓛ

212 477-0777

gramercytavern.com

Tavern: Sun–Th: 12pm–11pm,
Fri–Sat: 12pm–12am,
Main Dining: Mon–Th: 12pm–2pm,
    5:30pm–10pm,
Fri: 12pm–2pm, 5:30pm–11pm,
Sun: 5:30pm–10pm

Anthony's fare is less outré than Eleven Madison Park's, and solidly American. Excellent (and obscure) brews like Maine's Allagash Black are on draft, as were two organic reds by the glass, including a velvety Côtes du Rhône. This matched well with a delicious starter of merguez (all meats are antibiotic-free)—thin tubes of delicately spicy lamb floating in a supersavory broth, along with fresh chickpeas and split almonds. Also impressive was a silky, good-for-the-liver Jerusalem artichoke soup drizzled with beads of orange juice. Another appetizer—heirloom cauliflower—glowed royally purple, flaunting its vitamin-packed nature under a flurry of golden raisins and crunchy almonds. As per entrées, we were underwhelmed by undercooked chicken, but excited by grass-fed roast beef generously stuffed into foccacia and paired with a über-salubrious dandelion salad. The dandelion greens were the best we'd had anywhere, dressed simply in a creamy lemon dressing to temper their sharpness. Though no naturally sweetened desserts are to be found, sweet farewells from the charming hostess will follow you out the door—yet another reason Mom will love it.   ALEX VAN BUREN

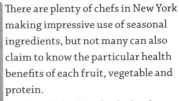

GREENSQUARE TAVERN

New American
5 W. 21st St.
(5th Ave. & Avenue of the Americas)

Ⓝ Ⓡ Ⓕ Ⓜ ④ ⑥

212 929-2468
greensquaretavern.com
See website for hours

There are plenty of chefs in New York making impressive use of seasonal ingredients, but not many can also claim to know the particular health benefits of each fruit, vegetable and protein.

Enter John Marsh, chef and managing partner at Greensquare Tavern, who's also a certified nutrition and lifestyle counselor. His Flatiron district restaurant features lovingly

worn blue-and-white tile floors, exposed brick walls, and tabletop plants in terra cotta pots. Marsh's plates convey a similar down-to-earth beauty; our roasted beet salad was a pretty tangle of arugula and frisee tossed in aged apple vinegar, with creamy Grand Reserve goat cheese and sweet cubes of roasted beet playing off the tart dressing and sliced hearts of palm. We eased into more fresh, seasonal produce next with a surprisingly substantial vegan cannellini and chickpea stew. Marsh adds swiss chard and kale to the broth—a flavorful base of garlic, shallot and spring herbs—just before serving to maintain texture and nutritional value. Kale also accompanied a plate of pan-seared Long Island Pekin duck breast with a slightly overpowering herbal red peppercorn glaze and stewed black cherries. Less intrusive was the nutty, iron-and-zinc-packed red rice served with the duck and with the skin-seared salmon that arrived next. Crisp green beans and subtle tarragon pan sauce cut refreshingly through the fatty sustainably-raised Loch Duart salmon. We paired it with a side of mashed sweet potatoes so vividly colored and, well, sweet, that we assumed agave or sugar must have been added—neither was, we learned, only butter. Dessert seemed gratuitous at that point, but we splurged anyway on Missouri organic pecan pie, made with raw honey instead of sugar for a mellow sweetness.

If Marsh continues serving dishes like these, he'll have no trouble convincing diners that taste, sustainability and health need not be mutually exclusive.

SARAH AMANDOLARE

NYC's Chelsea Market is admittedly a strange dining destination. The former Nabisco factory looms forbiddingly over several Chelsea blocks, evoking a sort of gothic hobbitville for adults. Traipse down an echoing, industrial hallway, where every crumbling, falling-apart brick-covered arch reveals a new artisanal food purveyor such as beloved local Amy's Breads or

GREEN TABLE @ CHELSEA MARKET
New American
75 9th Ave. @ 15th St.
① ② ③ Ⓐ Ⓒ Ⓔ Ⓛ
212 741-6623
cleaverco.com
Mon–Sat: 11:30am–4pm, 5pm–10pm,
Sun: 11am–4pm

antibiotic-free ice cream vendor Ronnybrook Farms. But among the best discoveries here is the heartbreakingly tasty burger at The Green Table. We took our seats at the communal table facing the mechanized "waterfall" in the main hallway. There, we eyeballed the daily-changing menu touting "fresh, seasonal, local, handcrafted" American classics. Nearly all of the mostly organic food was a success. Our burger was made of Empire State-raised, grass-fed beef and arrived plump on a roll from Amy's. Sweet tomato relish is lavished on top, along with couldn't-believe-it kimchi and the crispiest bacon we've tasted in ages. The result is a sweet/tart/salty combo that had us declaring this one of the best burgers we'd found. Not quite as thrilling was a grilled cheese; made with Neighborly Farms raw-milk cheddar, herb butter and apricot compote, we could taste only the cheese. Better was a substantial side salad of frisée tumbled with bright slices of orange. Bird-lovers, don't despair: There's a great free-range chicken potpie on offer here. Break the shiny, crackly pâte brisée crust to reveal moist slices of dark meat, corn and peas in a savory broth. It's available frozen for takeaway, or better yet, to stay with a crisp local draft.

ALEX VAN BUREN

GUSTORGANICS
Argentinean
519 Avenue of the Americas
(@ 6th Ave.)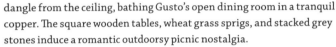
212 242-5800
gustorganics.com
Mon–Thu: 11am–11pm,
Fri–Sat: 11am–12am,
Sun: 11am–11pm

Planning a meal with your celiac, vegetarian, and diehard organic friends is no longer difficult. GustOrganics, NYC's only 100% certified organic restaurant and bar, is the knee-jerk recommendation for those seeking an eatery for all types of diets. The subdued décor even reflects the restaurant's benevolent green initiative without feeling too ambitious. Orange-tinged orbs

dangle from the ceiling, bathing Gusto's open dining room in a tranquil copper. The square wooden tables, wheat grass sprigs, and stacked grey stones induce a romantic outdoorsy picnic nostalgia.

Gusto's menu includes an impressive array of gluten-free, vegan, and carnivorous options in addition to the promise of a 100% organic meal, but remain open to compromise. The kitchen may fumble a dish or two, but the quality of the ingredients is steadily reliable. Any of the grass-fed beef specialties are a safe bet; Gusto's Argentine owners do their South American motherland justice with their perfectly juicy and crimson-centered filet mignon. Opt for resilient, char-kissed vegetables on the side but steer (pun intended) clear of the limp, strangely smoky kale. Snag a fruit smoothie—the pura vida is an attractive pale pink color and has a perfect icy consistency, its tangy strawberry delicately complemented by the smooth banana.

While some dishes are sure to please in both quality and taste, others toe the line. A special grilled pineapple salad's arugula and roasted red peppers' natural sweetness could have better complimented the fruit but instead were decidedly acrid. The fugazzeta and champignon pizza was tasty but weighed down beneath a heavy layer of caramelized onions. Both gluten-free and whole-wheat crusts are available for all pizzas, nudging us back in the direction of compromise. We wish that GustOrganics' dinners could be more consistently delicious, but the comfort of fresh, organic ingredients is enough to elicit return visits. ALLIX GENESLAW

If there's a more calm-inducing restaurant lurking near chaotic, shop-infested Herald Square, we haven't found it. This dreamlike Korean eatery comes with only one caveat: Be prepared to lose the shoes. A line of them marks the foyer, so kick 'em off, step up onto clean wooden boards, tread to your seat, and slip below-ground—or so it feels—to sit on slim cushions at a low table. Though this may sound high-maintenance, the zenlike

HANGAWI
Korean, Gourmet Vegetarian
12 E. 32nd St.
(5th and Madison Ave.)
⑥ Ⓑ Ⓓ Ⓕ Ⓜ Ⓝ Ⓠ Ⓡ
212 213-0077
hangawirestaurant.com
Mon–Thu: 12pm–2:45pm,
   5pm–10:15pm,
Fri: 12pm–2:45pm, 5pm–10:30pm,
Sat: 1pm–10:30pm,
Sun: 5pm–9:30pm

effect of the space—glowing orange walls, modern low-lit lighting fixtures, ornate Korean art—is that of an upscale yoga studio.

The all-vegan fare possesses equally sedative properties: A slim all-organic menu comes tucked into a "regular" menu. Among its wide-ranging offerings were a delicious dandelion and avocado salad with a peanuty wasabi sauce in which nutty dressing and buttery fruit nicely counter the bite of super-salubrious dandelion greens. We stuck to this menu as much as possible, and were equally impressed by its entrées. Mushrooms (present in most dishes) are scattered liberally through a brown rice-and-onion mixture served in a hot stone bowl. Bits of rice darken as they press up against the side of the bowl, so snag the proffered hot sauce to swirl through the whole, let it all keep cooking, and midway through your meal, start breaking crunchy bits off the side—they're addictive. Steamboat soup is—par for the course—pacifying: Clean, thin and aromatic as all get-out, slim oyster mushrooms contribute a woodsy flavor to the veggie-spiked broth. Tea here—fresh ginger strips floating in a giant mug with honey and a wedge of lemon—is unmissable. So get a pedicure, skip yoga and head to Hangawi. Just try not to nap. By meal's end Jared and I were both sprawling with eyes half-open, propping ourselves up against the wall—a rare happenstance in Gotham.   ALEX VAN BUREN

HENRY'S
New American
2745 Broadway (@ W. 105th St.) ①
212 866-0600
henrysnyc.com
Mon–Thu: 12pm–11pm,
Fri: 12pm–1am,
Sat: 11am–1am,
Sun: 11am–12am

"This place is really...not claustrophobic." My friend was right; Henry's is spacious. There's room to take in the mahogany digs without knocking into a waiter and to spread a few dishes across the picnic tablecloth. There's also room outside, where diners can take in Broadway behind the safety of a picket fence.

Henry's is a French bistro, modern American style; outsized and adorned with Herman Miller Company's "Summer Picnic" posters. The food is likewise an American take on bistro fare, generously portioned with global influences and mostly local ingredients. Hazelnuts wakened an otherwise dull salad of shredded kale with grapes and sliced endives. Jicama lent a welcome crunch to the gazpacho, a zesty puree of red and white peppers with jalapeno and mint.

Henry's pastas are discernibly fresh, made nearby with New York state flour. A summery tagliatelle saw chunks of Maine lobster—claws intact—tossed with wild mushrooms, Jersey tomatoes and arugula. Thankfully, the chef didn't mask the shellfish with seasoning and cream, and its flavor seeped into the gently buttered noodles. He showed equal command with the Long Island pork, an oven-roasted tenderloin dusted with sage and surrounded by white bean ragout, cherry tomatoes and wilted spinach in a light carrot, parmesan and brown butter sauce. The roasted vegetable entrée was equally satisfying. Every part of this dish was a highlight: thick wedges of zucchini, eggplant, fennel, onion and squash; wide, soft strips of red pepper; sweet slices of tomato; a fluffy heap of quinoa, cracked wheat and lentil; and a garlicky, smoky-sweet romesco sauce binding it all together.

Henry's may not be warm and cozy, but it's refreshingly approachable; there's plenty of room and gratifying food for everyone. And an everyday family menu (three courses for $14-20) makes it that much more welcoming for early diners.   JACLYN EINIS

On cobblestoned Cornelia street, Home is relatively unnoticeable to passersby. It's a real neighborhood charmer, tucked into a tiny space. Handsome wooden tables and chairs fill the room while small candles illuminate framed photos, and wine bottles are ferreted away in stray corners.

Locals dine on the small back patio under the canopy of trees and

HOME
New American
20 Cornelia St. (4th St. and 6th Ave.)

Ⓐ Ⓒ Ⓔ Ⓑ Ⓓ Ⓕ Ⓜ

212 243-9579
homerestaurantnyc.com
Mon–Fri: 11:30am–4pm, 5:00pm–11pm,
Sat: 10:30am–4pm, 5:30pm–11pm,
Sun: 10:30am–4pm, 5:30pm–10pm

the backs of brownstones. The menu is New American, showcasing local, sustainable, and seasonal ingredients—it reads like a road trip up the coast with stops in Hudson Valley, Lake Placid, and Nantucket.

The menu is meat-heavy but built on perfectly cooked and seasoned vegetables, which sometimes outshine the meat. A Mountain Dell Farms mixed green lettuce salad was true farm-to-table with shaved fennel, cucumber and a bold mustard-thyme vinaigrette, but a forgettable shredded duck salad needed some juice.

The menu changes often (sometimes substituting savory bread pudding for quinoa salad), so if the pretty blue corn crepes are on deck, surely order. Scattered with herbs and packed with mushrooms and peppers, they are a deliciously substantial vegetarian option. Carnivores will be happy with the hanger steak. It is full-flavored, grass-fed, and will give your jaw some action. A whole grilled brook trout, filleted at the table, has snowy-white flesh that is worth picking out any excess bones.

While the water isn't filtered, the all-American wine list is heavy on New York vintages and features a few biodynamic bottles and by-the-glass selections. Chef Ross Grill received some exposure on the Food Network show Chopped in August of 2010, so call to ensure a seat, but be warned; a full house will leave you elbow to elbow with the next table. After your meal, there's a plate of homemade chocolate chip cookies, to nibble on your way out; just like home.   SCARLETT LINDEMAN

HUDSON CLEARWATER

New American

447 Hudson St.
(Morton & Barrow St.)

Ⓐ Ⓑ Ⓒ Ⓓ Ⓔ Ⓕ Ⓜ ① ②

212 989-3255
hudsonclearwater.com
Mon–Fri: 12pm–3pm, 6pm–12am,
Sat–Sun: 10am–3pm, 6pm–12am

Hudson Clearwater's nearly hidden entrance justifies the existence of smart phones. There is neither a sign to advertise its name nor a window to display its attractive slate blue and exposed brick dining room. The only proper way to enter, though it feels entirely incorrect, is to stumble upon an enticing open gate and into the back garden. Needless to say, locating this popular West

Village spot without preliminary research or a trusty iPhone can be a befuddling affair. Once you're finally nestled into your indoor four-top (which can only be secured with a reservation), chef's counter barstool, or outdoor metal table (both available for walk-ins), you'll feel all the more deserving of the delicious meal to follow.

The refreshing watercress salad is perfectly suited to the garden setting. It is lightly coated with a tangy vinaigrette and accented with zesty goat cheese crumbles, sweet beet strips, and flecks of candied lemon. Be sure to order the outstanding butter clam and gnocchi appetizer. A summery fusion of clam chowder and mussels in classic white wine sauce, the clams, freckled gnocchi, and surprisingly crisp kale are served in a thin broth that brims with butter and lemon flavors. Both entrees we sampled, duck and hanger steak, featured tender, well-executed proteins. As a whole, I preferred the hanger steak dish due to its sides—a potato-onion gratin with a creamy interior and heaping portion of kale. The potatoes served alongside the duck had a nice crunch, though the chard was steeped in a jus that was slightly too salty for our tastes. After sampling the delicious menu, I'm hoping that the confusing whereabouts will help this excellent restaurant remain a well-kept secret.

ALLIX GENESLAW

Eating gets primitive as Hu Kitchen brings "food for humans" to Union Square. Influenced by the Paleo philosophy, this health-focused eatery features an entirely gluten-free menu of nutritious, whole foods without dairy and grains (unless specially noted). I walked into the spacious 5th Avenue locale to find an industrial-meets-natural interior with sleek

HU KITCHEN
Fast Food, New American, Paleo
78 5th Avenue (13th and 14th St.)
④ ⑤ ⑥ Ⓝ Ⓠ Ⓡ Ⓛ Ⓕ Ⓜ
212 510-8919
hukitchen.com
Mon–Fri: 7am–10pm,
Sat: 8am–10pm,
Sun: 9am–9pm

metallic details, tree trunk table tops and second floor loft-like seating.

A made-to-order meal area touts hormone-free meats and organic vegetables, often gathered from nearby Union Square Greenmarket. Bowls are a popular choice here. Create your own by selecting a base—organic quinoa, root vegetable mash or raw veggie medley—to top with roasted wild mushrooms, "Hu Joe" grass-fed ground beef flavored with tomato and spices, or robust organic Thai chicken: intensely flavorful pulled chicken simmered in coconut milk, turmeric, ginger, lemongrass, cilantro and basil.

Heartier lunch and dinner entrées include the tasty "Grandmaster Veg," which layers eggplant, carrot, green cabbage and housemade marinara in a lasagna-style casserole. Hormone-free rotisserie chicken brined in sea salt and dusted with organic coconut sugar was another standout with crisped skin and fall-off-the-bone meat. Seasonal soups and sides like charred, chili-kissed broccolini, roasted brussels sprouts, and caramelized pineapple wedges coated with cashew cream can be added to any dish.

Hu Kitchen offers dine-in and delivery seven days a week. Early morning options include a make-your-own breakfast mashbar with chia seed pudding and fruit and nut toppings, freshly baked muffins, and hot and cold cereals served with house-made almond milk or organic dairy. If you're on-the-go, pick up prepared foods like grass-fed New Zealand venison, wild line-caught albacore tuna salad, and curried sweet potatoes with organic dried apricots and almonds. With so many flavor options and high quality ingredients, "getting back to human" never tasted so good.

MEGAN MURPHY

HUNDRED ACRES
New American
38 Macdougal St.
(Prince & Houston St.)
① ⓒ Ⓔ Ⓝ Ⓡ Ⓑ Ⓓ Ⓕ Ⓜ ⑥
212 475-7500
hundredacresnyc.com
Mon–Fri: 12pm–4pm, 5:30pm–11pm,
Sat: 10:30am–3pm, 5:30pm–11pm,
Sun: 10:30am–3pm, 5:30pm–10pm

This newest member of the Cookshop/ Five Points trifecta boasts an identical husband-wife owner team and the same desire to source locally. The trendy West Village eatery also sports a see-and-be-seen bar area, with a dining room up front made slightly noisy by pretty white tiles lining the bar. Japanese-inspired lanterns hang overhead, French windows open to the street and a general sociable

buzz dominates—the back room or petite garden might be better for a sedate evening out.

I have dined here once before, and happily, the food has undergone a 360, with all the entrées and most of the appetizers impressing us both. Jared delighted in options for what he terms "healthy omnivores"—organic chicken, grass-fed beef, myriad fish and a selection of vegetables for those who don't eat meat (though veggie entrées were sadly lacking). Health-friendly sea salt graced the table, but happily, none of the food—whether a sweet slice of bluefish perched atop garlicky eggplant purée or a grilled pork chop matched with spicy peach "catsup"—required it. In fact, our fries were quite over-salted, but the staff quickly replaced them with those to our taste. Beet greens, of huge nutritional value, also made an appearance, and their dark leaves were toothsome and buttery.

Service, too, has much improved. Our bartender ably paired a Malbec—many wines here are organic or biodynamic—with a decadent chicken liver mousse. And as per burgers, this may be the time to add cheese. All-natural Pennsylvania-produced aged Goot Essa cheddar added a slightly earthy note to a downright juicy grass-fed burger. One caveat: A treviso-and-blackberry salad comprises eight slices of naturally tart treviso under an even more bitter berry dressing. So although the occasional misstep remains at Hundred Acres, by and large, the kitchen has gotten it together.   ALEX VAN BUREN

An out-of-towner calls and demands a proper introduction to New York dining—someplace "chic, European and very New York." Take him to Il Buco. The Italian eatery is almost dauntingly Old World, imbuing the throwaway adjectives "beautiful," "rustic" and "romantic" with real meaning via a visual cacophony of hanging copper pots,

IL BUCO
Italian
47 Bond St. (Bowery and Lafayette St.)
6 B D F M N R
212 533-1932
ilbuco.com
Mon–Thu: 12pm–11pm,
Fri–Sat: 12pm–12am,
Sun: 5pm–10:30pm

dark wooden antiques, profusions of flowers and whimsical metal light fixtures. We braced ourselves, for surely chef Ignacio Mattos couldn't compete with this level of charm. But he did, starting with knockout starters: A huge square of lasagna concealed spicy organic beef, kale and heady, gorgeous taleggio amidst its folds. Vegetable "carpaccio" of razor-thin zucchini and squash equally impressed, with a jolt of citrus juice, sparkles of mint and curls of salty parmesan. Perusing the menu while waiting for entrées, we noticed the restaurant's use of local purveyors, listed on its back like a starting lineup. Foodies and locavores alike will be impressed to see heavy hitters like upstate's Flying Pig Farm (bacon) and Ronnybrook Farms (milk). As per health, Il Buco gets high marks for sea salt, filtered water and organic animal products—though we wouldn't have minded seeing more dark greens on offer, especially with such hearty meats. Pork belly was extremely fatty (as is its wont), so trust the waitress when she emphasizes this or prepare to fill up on its sides of snappily fresh peas and soft white beans. Fish proved a better option that evening—a fillet of hake delivered lightly fried, crisp, and alongside a gorgeous array of heirloom red and yellow tomatoes for a bite of acidity. This is absolutely a date place, but call ahead and be sure you get your own table; it may be European to sit at a loud, jovial, communal table, but in the glow of candlelight, it's preferable to dine with just one other.

ALEX VAN BUREN

IL BUCO ALIMENTARI & VINERIA

Italian, Market
53 Great Jones St.
(Lafayette St. & Bowery)

Ⓑ Ⓓ Ⓕ Ⓜ Ⓝ Ⓡ ⑥

212 837-2622
ilbucovineria.com
Mon–Thu: 12pm–3pm, 6pm–12am,
Fri: 12pm–3pm, 6pm–1am,
Sat: 11am–3pm, 5:30pm–1am,
Sun: 11am–3pm, 5:30pm–11pm

For one of the most autentico Italian experiences around, get your appetite ready and head to Il Buco Alimentari & Vineria. NoHo's rustic market, salumeria, bakery, wine bar and restaurant is an extension of chef Ignacio Mattos' original Il Buco, located on adjacent Bond Street.

In the front Alimentari grocery section, you can purchase artisanal dry goods, cured meats, and freshly baked bread to enjoy at home. Or settle into the warm, cozy Vineria and restaurant to sample seasonal specialties featuring organic, local produce and proteins from eco-friendly farms—precisely crafted using traditional Italian methods. Varied individual and high communal tables invites sharing the love with friends—or making new ones. Belly up to a spot by the open kitchen for a front row view of the staff busily churning out delicacies.

While the atmosphere charms, the simple, straightforward cuisine is most likely to entice a repeat visit. Served with crusty, chewy Italian bread, the house-made ricotta is a must have starter. A pillow of soft curds garnished with sugar snap peas, toasted pine nuts, mint, granola and a swirl of honey offered an inviting sweet-savory sensation. Another knockout appetizer of Manila clams arrived resting in zesty roasted pepper and garlic broth, thick cubes of pancetta sprinkled throughout.

Vegetable contorni, charcuterie and fresh pastas, seafood and meats complete the menu. Try the delicate twirls of "busiate" pasta coated with almonds, anchovies, sun-ripened duana tomatoes and capers. For a heartier entrée, the signature spit-roasted short ribs presented large chunks of tender, peppery meat edged by darkened, chewy bark. They were both exceptional mains.

Offering breakfast, lunch and dinner, Il Buco Alimentari & Vineria is a solid choice for a romantic date night or breaking bread with a group. Make a reservation to guarantee prompt seating—then prepare to mangia.   MEGAN MURPHY

Situated along a corporate expanse of Park Avenue, Inside Park presents guests with a seating quandary—to sit inside the historic, vaulted cathedral or on the massive, romantic terrace? Both are equally airy—the interior's 30-foot ceiling ensures its openness—though the difference lies in the noise level. On a warm evening,

INSIDE PARK AT ST. BART'S
New American
325 Park Ave. (@ 50th St.) 6 E M
212 593-3333
insideparknyc.com
Mon–Fri: 11:30am–9:30pm,
Sat: 11:30am–9pm

the lively patio is hands-down the place to be. Whether you choose to eat in or out, rest assured that the excellent menu is a constant—it touts sustainable meals that are sourced from a featured list of farm suppliers.

The appetizers we sampled were available only seasonally and were superb. Watermelon gazpacho presented a sweeter alternative to the tomatoey standard but stayed true to its roots with ample cucumber, and the light cappellini was kept simple with a gentle touch of garlic, olive oil, and roasted tomatoes. Some seasonal dishes circulate more steadily than others. The grass-fed ribeye is such an entrée; though the aggressive charred flavor was a little overpowering for me, the sliced rounds were a perfect medium rare. Battered onions and lightly dressed greens accompany the tender, salt-studded steak. Wild salmon was more my speed. Its delicate middle was well cooked, though the salty accompanying greens could have lent a little seasoning to the blander squash and zucchini. The main dishes' bountiful inclusion of produce makes the menu's side offerings more or less ignorable. Those with a penchant for spontaneity and change will appreciate Inside Park's frequently updated menu, which promises a new, tasty meal (or two, or three) with each subsequent visit. Even in midtown Manhattan, there's something simple and outdoorsy about consuming this tasty, locally-grown food in an open-air setting. ALLIX GENESLAW

JIMMY'S NO. 43
New American
43 E. 7th St. (2nd and 3rd Ave.) ⑥ Ⓝ Ⓡ
212 982-3006
jimmysno43.com
Daily 5:30pm–12am

If monks lived in the East Village and needed a chill place to sip a microbrew and nosh on a locally sourced snack, they would head here. The hobbithole-like gastropub features vaulted ceilings, arched doorways and a cloistered, abbey-like feel. Located just below street level on a chill strip of East 7th Street, the heavy wooden furniture and slightly hushed atmosphere make it a surprisingly romantic watering hole, especially early in the evening.

Owner Jimmy Carbone is a major proponent of sourcing locally and organically whenever possible, and even earned the Slow Food Snail of Approval for his food's "quality, authenticity and sustainability." Not bad for a bar. Jimmy's has two things in spades: high-quality, mostly local and organic fare, and microbrews. So if you're going to drink beer, this is the place to do it. All-natural and local options are abundant, including Brooklyn's Sixpoint—I sampled one of their tasty, hoppy IPAs—and wonderful upstate New York brewery Captain Lawrence. As for international options, Jimmy suggests all-natural German beers as being among the friendliest to pair with food, which have none of the candied sugar that a Belgian ale like Chimay delivers.

Though celebrated chef Phillip Kirschen-Clark departed in August 2008, the new chef had everything on his menu under control when we stopped by: Non-gamey medallions of lamb came drizzled with an addictive mint-yogurt sauce, and an heirloom tomato salad was among the best we sampled, with bright disks of tomato resting on a pillow of sweet, locally made ricotta and mozzarella di bufala. Overdone burger sliders were less impressive, but a farro salad speckled with radicchio and curls of preserved lemon was sprightly, and a nice nod to vegetarians. All in all, the monks have it good at Jimmy's.

ALEX VAN BUREN

Josie's occupies the medium-fancy end of the Louis Lanza dining continuum with tubular, sparkly lights providing refracted ambiance along the span of floor-to-ceiling windows and sunny yellow walls. Pan-American eats are intended for vegetarians and carnivores alike, with a menu featuring mostly organic produce, all antibiotic-free meats and an emphasis on sourcing locally. We squeezed in and

JOSIE'S
New American
300 Amsterdam Ave. (@ 74th St.)
① ② ③ Ⓑ Ⓒ
212 769-1212
Mon–Thu: 12pm–11pm,
Fri: 12pm–12am,
Sat: 11am–12am,
Sun: 11am–10pm

found that—though this isn't a date place; the service is a bit wonky and the neighboring conversations can be loud—it's obviously a neighborhood place, if the stream of chattering customers is any indication. They come for the food as well as the fine wine list, which included a number of sustainable and organic vinos. I went with a swell rosé crémant—a sparkling French wine—and was not disappointed.

We liked, but didn't love our meal: The best thing we tried was a starter of pan-seared black bean dumplings in a sweet mango sauce, though pumpkin soup drizzled with pesto was a fine nod to the leaves falling outside. Organic chicken was not the most flavorful, but it certainly had size on its side: A giant breast and thigh dwarfed the plate, and accompanied prettily julienned carrots and zucchini. Plump pieces of grass-fed strip steak proved fairly tasty served with lightly sautéed bok choy, and a tuna burger was lent oomph by wasabi mayo and pickled ginger. Skip optional sides of dull smashed potatoes and instead tuck into (more healthful) air-baked fries or sweet potatoes. We would have loved to end on a sweet note, but found that—though wheat- and dairy-free options were on tap—none were naturally sweetened. We'll cross our fingers that Josie will add this to her epic menu. ALEX VAN BUREN

KAIA WINE BAR
South African, Wine Bar
1614 3rd Ave. (90th St. & 91st St.)
④ ⑤ ⑥
212 722-0490
kaiawinebar.com
Mon–Thu: 5pm–12am,
Fri–Sat: 5pm–12:30am,
Sun: 5pm–11pm

With a multitude of restaurants at our fingertips, New Yorkers are often asked, "What type of food are you in the mood for?" While South African may not be a common response, Kaia Wine Bar might just ingrain this cuisine into your arsenal of go-tos. This darling Upper East Side restaurant offers seasonal South African-inspired small plates in a rustic, 50-seat setting.

Kaia, which means "home" in Zulu, is a candlelit neighborhood gem that's perfect for a romantic date night or fun evening out with friends. Focused solely on authentic South African flavors, chef Ivan Giani's eclectic menu features biodynamic and grass-fed meats, organic produce, local cheeses and a sustainable fish program. Beverages include South African and New World wines, along with a selection of American craft beers.

A starter of wild boar sliders topped with smoked tart cherry compote set the tone for an intensely flavorful meal. Along a narrow plate, creamy scoops of ostrich tartare alternated with watermelon radish slices and toast rounds over white chocolate mustard; the myriad of tastes and textures really impressed us when assembled together. Chilled tilefish ceviche mingled with diced kiwi fruit, oranges, red peppers and lime juice for a citrusy and refreshing warm weather dish, best enjoyed when spooned onto the accompanying crisped bread for added texture. Other meal highlights include the vibrant "Jacob's Nootjes" scallops atop sweet corn purée peppered with mango relish, and the savory "Spear and Shield" dish: bacon-wrapped asparagus resting on portobello mushrooms smothered in cheddar cheese and a rich green peppercorn sauce.

Will I be craving South African cuisine on a regular basis now? Absolutely. The delicious, high quality cuisine and cozy, unpretentious atmosphere make me want to call Kaia my new home away from home on the UES. MEGAN MURPHY

"Italian food is comforting" is a ubiquitous truism, but in a town full of glitzy eateries, jam-packed vino-by-the-glass bars, and subpar red sauce joints, it can be tricky to pinpoint a heart-warming Italian trattoria. Happily, there's Lupa. The West Village restaurant co-owned by Mario Batali has been churning out excellent Old World fare for

LUPA
Italian
170 Thompson St.
(Houston & Bleecker St.)
Ⓒ Ⓔ Ⓑ Ⓓ Ⓕ Ⓜ Ⓝ Ⓡ ① ⑥
212 982-5089
luparestaurant.com
Sun–Thu: 11:30am–11pm,
Fri–Sat: 11:30am–12am

many years. Don't let its hubbub dissuade you from eating there. Make a reservation or arrive early as a walk-in; you can always linger at the bar to admire the exposed brick interior and European feel of the place over a glass of vino selected from the extensive wine list.

To cut the wait, consider the long wooden communal table by the front: There's plenty of elbow room, and a chance to ask a neighbor about those beets drizzled with cream sauce and speckled with pistachios (they're worth it) or the roast summer squash aromatic with thyme and mint (even better). Save plenty of room for Lupa's buzzed-about pasta. The famous gnocchi was, on this one visit, stuffed with sausage and fennel, and it was good, but we enjoyed the basic pomodoro (tomato sauce) spaghetti even more. Batali's classic onion, carrot and thyme base makes for a surprisingly sweet sauce, and gets a spicy edge from chili pepper flakes. As for entrées, though fish is fine—skate was pleasantly buttery, and served with fried caper berries—we liked the (all antibiotic-free) meat the best. Pork shoulder was prepared using autumnal herbs like clove and nutmeg, but not to potpourri-like cloyingness; its deep-brown skin was crunchy, sweet and addictive, and the meat itself unbelievably moist. Small coins of steak arrived beautifully rosy, with a charred, dark ring, and were tender as could be—which is how we felt about Lupa after our meal. ALEX VAN BUREN

MAIALINO

Italian

2 Lexington Ave.
(Gramercy Park N. & 22nd St.)

④ ⑥ Ⓝ Ⓡ

212 777-2410
maialinonyc.com
Mon–Thu: 7:30am–10am, 12pm–2pm,
    5:30pm–10:30pm,
Fri: 7:30am–10am, 12pm–2pm,
    5:30pm–11pm,
Sat: 10am–2pm, 5:30pm–11pm,
Sun: 10am–2pm, 5:30pm–10:30pm

Maialino, an airy trattoria in the Gramercy Park Hotel, boasts an impressive pedigree. Owned by prolific restaurateur Danny Meyer, the Roman-style kitchen is led by a bold young chef named Nick Anderer.

You wouldn't know it walking inside, however, as the ample dining room feels friendly and casual. Market-style bread and antipasti stations flank the bar, and loads of natural light spills onto a yellow-tiled floor and across blue-checkered tablecloths. Chef Anderer skipped formal training and instead spent significant time eating and cooking in Rome. He honed an appreciation for traditional dishes and preparations, like classic cacio e pepe (pasta with pecorino and black pepper) and vegetables cooked with olive oil and garlic, chili or lemon. Fresh, high-quality ingredients are key to such simple dishes, and appropriately, Anderer is ardent about the sustainable farms he sources from.

We began with a good example of his appreciation for produce: a refreshing antipasto of insalata di sedano with thinly sliced celery and fennel, topped with crunchy roasted hazelnuts and grated, slightly sweet piave cheese. It took several bites to get a proper sense of each texture involved in the salad, keeping us fully engaged. Our first entrée was also texturally satisfying: a classic Trentino-style vignarola of firm fava beans and sweet peas accompanying a suitably springtime grilled sturgeon. We went in a heartier direction next, digging into the restaurant's namesake dish, malfatti al maialino: wide noodles in a suckling pig ragu, finished with scattered fresh arugula leaves. Despite its rich ingredients, the dish had lightness and subtlety of flavor and texture, with the peppery greens cutting through the pleasant fattiness of the ragu. Likewise, a dish of lamb chops and chard alla romana had a certain tough-meets-tender flair, as the hefty chops had an unexpectedly delicate black pepper and olive oil crust. Like Rome itself, Maialino's menu is reliably traditional yet capable of surprises.

SARAH AMANDOLARE

Buoyantly friendly service, organic bottles of wine around the twenty-four dollar mark, and Asian-inflected fare are the unexpected hallmarks of this Upper West Side restaurant. A neighborhood standby, the largely vegetarian eatery seems almost to have been

MANA
Asian, Macrobiotic
646 Amsterdam Ave. (91st & 92nd St.)
① ② ③
212 787-1110
manarestaurantnyc.com
Daily 11:30am–10:30pm

airdropped from the East Village. But no matter: The grub is good, the water filtered, and for health-conscious locals, the mostly organic menu is a gem of a discovery.

Ignore the slightly spartan decor—plain wooden tables strewn haphazardly around the room—and focus on the food. An aromatic miso-based vegetable soup delivers a hearty autumnal oomph via a few skinny wood ear mushrooms and *okonomoyaki*—our cheery waiter laughed as we struggled to pronounce it—a savory Japanese buckwheat pancake, is delicately fried up and served with sweet sundried tomato sauce. Pescatarians will delight in a number of fish options: Six crop up on the menu. We quite liked the frequent special of wild cod, flaky and moist, and served with a simple tamari-and-ginger glaze and a side of creamed millet. Though it may not sound crave-worthy, the millet will please polenta-lovers; the golden, smooth grain resembles that Italian staple in taste, and is the consistency of creamy mashed potatoes. But perhaps the best part of dining here are the many vegetable options: Bok choy and broccoli sautéed with ginger and garlic may sound run-of-the-mill, but it has a crispness and freshness that calls to mind a jaunt through the garden. As for the sugar-free desserts, none wowed us completely, though a fruit crisp dessert was decent. As you clear your plate, look around the spic-and-span joint, let the owner know how you liked the fare (she often tours the room to ask each diner) and note that she is cleaning the tables herself. It's just that sort of place.

ALEX VAN BUREN

MANZO (EATALY)
Italian
200 5th Ave. (23rd St. & 24th St.)
646 398-5100
eatalyny.com
Mon–Fri: 11:30am–4:30pm, 5pm–10pm,
Sat–Sun: 11:30am–10pm

Everyone who enters this culinary emporium—even the most jaded New Yorker—regresses into a state of doe-eyed fascination the minute he or she crosses the 5th Avenue threshold. There is so much to consume, both literally and visually, as everything—

from the celebrity owners and 50,000-square foot size to the extensive selection of both hyper local and imported foods—is over-the-top. Mario Batali, Joe Bastianich, and Lidia Bastianich teamed up with Oscar Farinetti to recreate his Turin, Italy original here in Manhattan. The result is a glorified warehouse cramped with almost every type of gourmet purveyor imaginable: coffee, gelato, panini, cured meat, fish, fresh pasta, housemade cheese, and pastries, to name a few.

Dining options abound, but Manzo is Eataly's only table service restaurant. Securing a table may be difficult, so a more impromptu, mix-and-match meal from the various vendors (like the pescateria, veggie plate station, and roasted meat and rotisserie poultry stands) is another viable option. Cafe seating, benches, and counters are provided for group-friendly dining. Like its retail-based counterparts, Manzo also serves sustainable, locally sourced produce and proteins and is masterful at vegetable incorporation and seasoning. My two favorite presentations are the heirloom tomatoes, wax beans, and zucchini that compose the sherry-dressed insalata stagione and the pureed, roasted, and shaved carrots that add sweet and savory flair to its fat-marbled pork rounds. The buttery, smoky tortelloni are transcendental; each resilient pouch is stuffed with milky cheese and topped with crisp pancetta cubes and earthy chanterelles. Don't overlook the menu's side offerings though. Dandelion greens interspersed with fleshy cannellini beans and salty pancetta are particularly hearty. When the meal is finished and you're thrust back onto Eataly's crowded floor, it's nice to know all the necessary ingredients for recreating Manzo's delicious dishes are conveniently at your disposal.   ALLIX GENESLAW

Marc Forgione, spawn of local food movement instigator Larry Forgione, styled his self-referential TriBeca restaurant as a farmhouse-fine dining hybrid. Tarnished saucepans, splintered wood shelves, and mismatched housewares contribute to the hokey, rural aesthetic, while the exposed brick walls, dim candlelight, and dark tables compose the chicer, more romantic half.

MARC FORGIONE
New American
134 Reade St. (@ Hudson St.)
① ② ③ Ⓐ Ⓒ Ⓔ
212 941-9401
marcforgione.com
Mon–Sat: 5pm–11:30pm,
Sun: 11am–2:30pm, 5pm–10pm

The menu's self-explanatory headings, "to start", "to follow", and "to share", enable it to flow efficiently, but its random usage of quotation marks may cause some head-scratching. Don't be deterred by the confusing punctuation—fluke "ravioli" may employ a noodle that more closely resembles lasagna, but the creative dish is delicious nonetheless. The wide, thin dough blankets the fully intact, tender filet and is topped with zucchini and a pesto drizzle. The grass-fed steak is well-cooked and lightly topped with a Maytag blue cheese butter, though its sweet, blueberry-infused jus is a little heavy-handed. The lamb chop is one of the tastiest dishes I've sampled recently. It incorporates Mediterranean flavors with feta cheese, sun-dried tomatoes, and black olive salt, but the orzo was questionably seeping in an unnecessary layer of oil. Since entrees could include more vegetable sides, it's wise to order some additional ones from the "to start" menu section. I'd recommend the "BLT", an heirloom tomato concoction whose playful use of pig ears lends smokiness to its sauce. Also reliable are the Greenmarket vegetables and lettuce, which combine radishes, zucchini, squash, and greens beneath a thin, creamy dressing. The menu may have to smooth out a few minor kinks, but Marc Forgione promises a well-rounded, sustainable meal in an intimate, attractive space.   ALLIX GENESLAW

MAS (FARMHOUSE)

New American, French
39 Downing St. (Bedford & Varick St.)
① Ⓐ Ⓒ Ⓔ Ⓑ Ⓓ Ⓕ Ⓜ PATH
212 255-1790
masfarmhouse.com
Daily: 6pm–11:30pm

This willfully cloistered restaurant is in the heart of Greenwich Village, a part of town that by its very topography feels top-secret, as high heels echo on quiet cobblestone streets. Push open the heavy wooden door to find an elegant, low-ceilinged homage to a French farmhouse ("Mas" is the Provençal word for it). Though we haven't yet seen a farmhouse with such an elegant bar space—five leather-covered stools, a cozy sitting area—and such pristinely white tablecloth-covered tables in the small formal dining area, we're sure there's such a thing somewhere.

The largely organic menu sources very close to home, which should please locavores, and seasonally changing fare is at its best brilliant and at worst, still quite good. Caveat emptor: The eaves of this "farmhouse" hang low, so ask for the corner table or compete with your neighbors for conversational rights. The chef offers two prix-fixe tastings, and—judging by the slightly finer cuts of meat in the identical dishes we ordered landing on the table next to us—it's possible he prefers preparing these. Even if you select à la carte, note that chef Galen Zamarra, who trained in France, does beautifully by seafood: His starter of basil sorbet, shredded crab and a tomato-water consommé tasted like—well, like falling in love. The sorbet melted effortlessly into the consommé bath, adding a tint of sweetness, and pale strands of crab were tender as could be. A starter of tuna tartare was seared to rare and covered with curls of salty crispy shallots, and an entrée of striped bass arrived with punchy, sweet corn. The sole disappointment was the duck, which we had to saw through—never a good sign. So go fishing, as it were, try not to eavesdrop on the stock-trading habits of fellow diners, and note that the staff has surreptitiously put The Who on the stereo. This farmhouse, it seems, is open to all of us. ALEX VAN BUREN

In Provincial France, a Mas is known as a country farmhouse that grows all the products to nourish the estate onsite. Though located in the heart of the West Village, Mas (la grillade) seeks out seasonal ingredients from small, organic and sustainable farms in communities surrounding New York City—thus forming their "estate."

MAS (LA GRILLADE)
New American
28 7th Ave. South (Leroy & Morton St.)
Ⓐ Ⓑ Ⓒ Ⓓ Ⓔ Ⓕ Ⓜ ⓵
212 255-1720
maslagrillade.com
Daily: 11:30am–2:30pm, 6pm–11:30pm

Since 2004, chef Galen Zamarra has been a leader in farm-to-table dining at Mas (farmhouse), his first WV establishment. Utilizing his years of experience, farmer connections and sustainable approach to fine dining, Galen opened Mas (la grillade) in late 2011. He showcases a seasonal menu of locally grown, sustainably raised foods cooked solely over fires of oak, apple and other hardwoods. When you open the Seventh Avenue South doors, you'll be greeted by the sweet fragrance of smoky, burning wood. A small bar and glass-walled wine room open into an elegant split-level dining room filled with wood tables, white tablecloths and a bright skylight ceiling.

The prix fixe and à la carte menu debuts fresh starters, like my salad of sliced roasted beets, pickled onions, marinated cucumbers and velvety smoked ricotta. Precise fire-grilled preparations let the flavors and beautiful qualities of the ingredients shine in each dish. An entrée of grilled duck presented succulent smoky medallions, rimmed with a thin layer of fat beneath the skin, plated over tender Swiss chard. Perfectly seared scallops laid atop a bed of grilled fennel and spring greens, drizzled with vibrant saffron-dill aioli. A subtle smokiness permeated every element on the plate; it was lovely.

Grilled vegetables, like wild ramps and hen of the wood mushrooms, along with fruit-based desserts, artisanal cheeses and house-made ice creams complete the menu. Creamy ricotta and local honey ice creams were already melting when placed on our table; nonetheless, they provided a tangy, refreshing finish to an overall wonderful meal.

MEGAN MURPHY

THE MEATBALL SHOP
Italian, American
Multiple Locations (see website)
themeatballshop.com

Naming a restaurant after a single item can be a tricky endeavor—yet the Meatball Shop confirms there is an exception to every rule. This no-fuss restaurant from co-owners Daniel Holzman and Michael Chernow elevates meatballs with ingredients like fennel seeds, prosciutto, and ricotta.

Sitting down at a sturdy, wooden table I couldn't ignore giddy expressions of fellow diners experimenting with playful flavor combinations. Jars of markers and laminated menus set a whimsical tone as I colored between the lines, pairing a classic beef herb-packed meatball with a chili-laced tomato sauce and a hearty veggie ball of green lentils with a thick mushroom gravy. Right as the volume of choices seemed overwhelming, our cheery server broke down the dishes, defining the quirky (and sometimes suggestive) names.

First up: naked balls. This is a meatball classicist's dream—nuances of heat and herb shine through in four unadorned meatballs. I was transported back to my grandmother's Italian kitchen with the 'smash' sandwich—two meatballs smashed inside toasted brioche. A word of caution: order this when eating with the kind of company that won't mind sauce dribbling down your chin. Butter lettuce, sweet-roasted parsnips, chickpeas, and you guessed it—meatballs—combine to form the vibrant 'everything but the kitchen sink salad'. We raved about flawless sliders including chicken and pesto. Side dishes were a bright counterpoint to hearty meat dishes, such as a lightly-dressed arugula and sliced apple salad or crisp steamed broccoli.

I would have preferred a two-top instead of squeezing into the center of a communal table—but one bonus was feasting our eyes on neighbor's selections. Ingredient-conscious customers can happily devour beef from Creekstone Farm and Heritage pork. The Meatball Shop's delicious food and whimsical atmosphere reminded me that sometimes, it's perfectly delightful to play with my food.   JESSICA COLLEY

With its worn-in wood, cushiony barstools, vintage Hudson River maps and Union Jack flag, Monument Lane feels decidedly homespun. The catch? Sophisticated food. The small plates and mains we sampled here were so layered with comforting, memorable yet worldly flavors, that we decided this place could be the perfect marriage of familiarity and unexpectedness – Mom's kitchen meets the West Village.

MONUMENT LANE
New American
103 Greenwich Ave. (W. 12th & Jane St.)
Ⓐ Ⓒ Ⓔ ① ② ③ Ⓛ
212 255-0155
monumentlane.com
Mon: 5:30pm–10:30pm,
Tue–Wed: 12pm–3pm, 5:30pm–11pm,
Thu–Fri: 12pm–3pm, 5:30pm–11:30pm,
Sat: 11am–4pm, 5:30pm–12am,
Sun: 11am–4pm, 5:30pm–10:30pm

The menu includes oysters, cheese and butcher boards, and "bites," like toasts topped with smoked fish and snack-able blistered Shishito peppers, but we skipped right to the "small plates," essentially appetizers for two. The BLT Salad was our favorite dish of the night, a knockout combination of salt and freshness. Thick slices of green heirloom tomatoes were set atop a long oval plate and topped with quartered red heirlooms, arugula, generous pieces of house-smoked bacon and a fresh basil aioli. Monument Lane sources from regional sustainable farms and changes up its menu weekly to reflect what's fresh; the salad was a delicious example of this practice.

Our first main course, grilled swordfish, was nicely charred and fork-tender, served alongside a spicy pureed eggplant and sliced grape tomatoes. A bit of quinoa and basil topped the fish for added Italian flavor and texture. Next, we dug into a juicy roasted half chicken with a Moroccan bent, by way of firm basmati rice tossed with chickpea salad – a mix of delfino cilantro, sweet black currants and Manzanilla olives. A stripe of smooth, mellow saffron yogurt sauce lined the plate, alongside a grilled lemon. To finish the evening, we shared a simple dessert of sweet macerated peaches and airy whipped cream over a thick triangle of corn cake. Our craving for fresh produce sated, we strolled away from our sidewalk table into the breezy night.   SARAH AMANDOLARE

MULBERRY AND VINE

New American, Fast Food
73 Warren St. (W Broadway &
Greenwich St.)

① ② ③ ④ ⑤ ⑥ Ⓐ Ⓒ Ⓔ

212 791-6300
Mon–Fri: 7:30am–8:30pm,
Sat: 9am–5pm

"Eat Local, Cook Global" is the mantra at new Tribeca eatery, Mulberry & Vine. Inside the casual café on Warren Street is a clean and spacious two-story interior with a walk up counter and upstairs seating loft with reclaimed wood tables. Health-conscious eaters can drop by for an internationally inspired breakfast, lunch, and light fare from Monday - Saturday.

Here, it's all about letting the best, highest quality ingredients shine. Dairy, eggs and tofu are organic and local; greens and grains too, when possible and in season. All poultry and meats are hormone- and antibiotic-free; sauces and dressings are made in house without preservatives. And instead of loading up foods with fats and oils, chef Justin Schwartz and team use local pesticide-free herbs and spices to elevate flavors.

Ordering your meal is simple: select any combination of the prepared hot and cold dishes that you desire. Then you can add a bed of seasonal greens or one of the daily soups, like chipotle gazpacho or African tomato curry. Global flavors were apparent in the turkey meatballs spiced with garam masala, ginger, and jalapeño. The signature skin-on roasted chicken seasoned with lemon and rosemary was juicy and robust, but the vegetarian enchiladas were my lunchtime winner, with thinly sliced vegetables layered amongst peppery tomatillo poblano yogurt sauce. They were delicious. Be sure to inquire about the daily farmer's market specials, too.

A slew of prepared salads and snacks like homemade curried cashews are available to grab on-the-go. Beverage options include blended fruit and veggie juices from LuliTonix, Laughing Man coffee, and wines from Channing Daughters.

The Mulberry & Vine team is passionate about what they do and it translates to the flavorful food they serve. Do good for both your body and mind and drop by next time you're in the 'hood.   MEGAN MURPHY

If you don't want to break the bank before that Lincoln Center play or Central Park ramble, put Nanoosh on your radar. The humble chickpea is the focus of this hummus-centric eatery, with the beige bean making a starring appearance in dangling glass light fixtures as well as all across the menu. Nanoosh has been offering "fresh, organic, natural" fare since they opened in 2008 and since then has expanded to multiple locations across the city. Most, though not all, of the produce is organic, and all of the meat is hormone- and antibiotic-free.

Hummus here is for those who like a super-tahini edge and almost peanut-butter like consistency to the classic Mediterranean dish. Though freshly made, it's very thick, and not always my bag—I preferred the version topped with spicy, crumbled beef that, along with a few toasted pine nuts, effectively cut its density. Even better were wraps, particularly chicken: lean strips of the bird tucked into a thin, handmade wheat wrapper and speckled with organic onions, greens and tahini. Salads were a bit hit or miss: an über-healthy quinoa salad was packed with juicy raisins and bits of pepper, and is available as a side. But the Nanoosh green salad is almost 70% carrots—no joke when they say it's grated on top—and we found little relief from the tart arugula in either of the citrus dressings offered. But Jared was pleased to see digestion-aiding mint in my delicious, brown sugar-sweetened lemonade, and I was happy to see several varieties of popular Peak's Organic Ale on offer. Perhaps the best aspect of Nanoosh—a fine discovery for those who left their picnic planning to the last minute—is that their uptown locations deliver to Central Park. Hummus on demand: gotta love New York.   ALEX VAN BUREN

NANOOSH
Mediterranean, Hummus Bar
2012 Broadway (68th St. & 69th St.)
212 362-7922 ① ② ③ Ⓑ Ⓒ
Sun–Wed: 11am–10pm,
Th–Sat: 11am–11pm

111 University Pl. (12th St. & 13th St.)
212 387-0744 ④ ⑤ ⑥ Ⓝ Ⓡ Ⓠ Ⓛ
Sun–Tue: 11am–10pm,
Wed–Sat: 11am–11pm

173 Madison Ave. (33rd St. & 34th St.)
212 447-4345 ④ ⑥
Mon–Fri: 11am–9pm, Sat: 11am–6pm
nanoosh.com

NAYA EXPRESS
Mediterranean, Fast Food
688 Third Ave. (43rd St. & 44th St.)

④ ⑤ ⑥ ⑦ Ⓢ

212 557-0007
nayarestaurants.com
Mon–Fri: 11am–10pm

The tomatoes at Lebanese fast food spot Naya Express taste like tomatoes. The arugula tastes deliciously bitter, and the finely chopped flat leaf parsley, generously doused on, well, everything, has that characteristically crackly texture.

This revelation—vegetables tasting like vegetables—is thanks to Baldor, the fine food purveyor in the Bronx that sources mostly from farms in the Northeast. These delicious vegetables adorn every menu offering. The halal meats (indicating the animals are fed a vegetarian diet and slaughtered humanely) are from De Bragga and Spitler, a legendary NYC butcher known for quality and naturally raised proteins. The kitchen produces juicy chicken shawarma, chicken taouk and beef kebabs, falafel, and some incarnation of ground lamb (in an excellent hand-made sausage kebab called "sujuk" here)—all delivered in a whole-wheat or white pita wrap, vermicelli-adorned rice or salad bowl and finished with whatever toppings and sauces you point to (pickled turnips, garlic whip, tahini, spicy red sauce, and jalapeno are among the myriad of housemade options).

The quality sourcing pays off; the food is really excellent. Hummus is rich and creamy, the baba ganoush smoky and smooth. The chicken and beef kebabs, while sometimes a touch dry (saved easily by a drizzle of the olive oil conveniently placed on the tables), are seasoned perfectly, and the lamb sausage is heady with aromatic flavor and lip-smacking juiciness.

Unfortunately, none of this is a secret. The lines at Naya Express are very long. But the staff moves quickly, so don't be discouraged—just plan accordingly.

TALIA BERMAN

There is something futuristic about Naya, so the fact that Naya means "new" in Arabic comes as no surprise. There is a mysterious and serene vibe conveyed by the dramatic lighting and the light patter of the staff as they tend to their guests. The restaurant

NAYA MEZZE AND GRILL
Mediterranean
1057 Second Ave. (@ 56th St.) Ⓔ Ⓜ
212 319-7777
nayarestaurants.com
Mon–Fri: 12pm–10pm,
Sat: 12:30pm–10:30pm,
Sun: 12:30pm–9:30pm

is impossibly narrow, made more so by the strange design of each table (built literally into the wall). A walk to the end of the darkish "hallway" reveals a bigger room with skylights and a communal table that feels a bit like the white light at the end of the tunnel. The kitchen is initially nowhere to be found; upon closer inspection, however, I can glimpse the kitchen behind a window covered with white blinds. What secrets are they protecting behind those shades?

Quite a few, it seems. A spinach salad with onion, tomato, walnut and pomegranate-citrus dressing bridges the sweet-savory divide with great success. Their selection of mezze, adds "muhammara," a sweet and nutty red pepper dip, to the usual suspects of hummus, tabbouleh and baba ganoush. Be aware, though; the chef is not afraid to use garlic and zaatar (a blend of Middle Eastern herbs and spices). The real apex of the meal came with the grilled Australian lamb chops—incredibly flavorful and perfectly juicy at medium-rare. We were happy to discover that all lamb and beef are grass-fed and chicken is naturally-raised. However, the "Samké Harra," a broiled striped bass topped with spicy tahini, walnut and pine nuts is underwhelming and desperately lacks acid—but this was one misstep among many successes.

The food is more carefully prepared and presented than any Lebanese restaurant I have ever been to; the staff at Naya clearly knows what they are doing, and, for the most part, they execute it well.

TALIA BERMAN

NICK AND TONI'S CAFÉ

Italian, Mediterranean
100 West 67th St. (Broadway &
Columbus Ave.) ① ② ③ Ⓑ Ⓒ
212 296-4000
nickandtoniscafe.com
Mon–Fri: 12pm–3:30pm,
   5:30pm–10:30pm,
Sat: 12pm–3:30pm, 5pm–10:30pm,
Sun: 11:30am–3:30pm, 5pm–10pm

For an unassuming restaurant in the shadows of Lincoln Center, Nick and Toni's Cafe is making some serious food. This location is the city offshoot of the eponymous East Hampton Nick and Toni's, both serving rustic Mediterranean fare showcasing organic and sustainable foods on a menu that changes with the seasons. Many daily specials feature vegetables from the NYC Greenmarkets and Ronnybrook Farms (only 2 hours outside the city) provides all the dairy.

In the dimmed fresco-laden dining room, theatregoers tuck into lakes of risotto and sip North Fork merlot. The wood-burning oven anchors the room, sending out toasted pizzas at lunch—during which they also offer more casual fare, including a juicy grass-fed dry-aged Black Angus hamburger.

On the evening we dined, a salad special was a winning combination of perfectly dressed roasted beets, mache, and ricotta salata. However, our rigatoni with cotechino sausage and pepperoncino was blazingly spicy in bites and too salty in others.

We were most impressed by the entrees, and the real pleasure lies in their simplicity. Branzino with snap peas is just that—perfectly cooked fish with a generous portion of lightly blanched peas that taste of spring. The kitchen uses light seasonings like high quality olive oil, sea salt, and lemon, allowing the flavors of the vegetables to shine through. A juicy Griggstown Farms poussin was well-matched with heaps of grilled asparagus and oven roasted tomatoes. If the plentiful vegetables next to the proteins still aren't enough, there are always half a dozen vegetable sides like local pea shoots and wilted greens to ensure your five-a-day.

Visit Nick and Toni's Cafe for a quick pre-theater bite or a leisurely dinner; either way, Upper West Side diners can enjoy delicious Mediterranean food they can feel great about eating—without the trek to the Hamptons. SCARLETT LINDEMAN

Named after one of New York's oldest heirloom apples, Northern Spy Food Co. is an East Village eatery from San Francisco expats built on fine cooking, sustainably raised meats, whole grains, and loads of charm. Shelves in the back are stocked with locally made pickles, and the tabletops have been repurposed from old wooden bowling alley lanes. The cerulean-blue slated banquettes wrap around the room, fostering a warm and cozy atmosphere.

NORTHERN SPY FOOD CO.
New American
511 East 12th St. (Ave. A & Ave. B) Ⓛ
212 228-5100
northernspyfoodco.com
Mon–Fri: 10am–4pm, 5:30pm–close,
Sat–Sun: 10am–3:30pm,
5:30pm–close

The smallish menu champions ingredients produced by regional farmers and artisan purveyors. Chef Nathan Foot is at the helm, receiving full sides of organic Fleisher's pork weekly and transforming them into brined and grilled loin steaks, roasted aromatic porchettas, and succulent pork terrines. Northern Spy features local craft beers Kelso and Sixpoint on tap, and New York wines. Red Jacket Ciders and homemade seltzer flavored with blood orange and lemon-lime round out the drink menu.

The food menu is loosely organized into salads, starches, and proteins, with unique snacks and sides filling it out—think pickled eggs, red quinoa, and even a wild rice with local feta, mint, and lemon. Everything on the menu feels light; even the marinara-drenched meatballs we sampled can be best described as porky clouds. Freekeh risotto, a stubborn green wheat loaded with fiber, is melted into submission and, when we dined, was dotted with delicious cubes of butternut squash. The dishes are satisfying and thoughtful and often feature unique touches; for example, the addition of crispy black rice on a mess of squid and white beans added a delightful crunch.

With such charismatic food and an utterly alluring venue, if I lived in the East Village, I'd make Northern Spy Food Co. my second home.

SCARLETT LINDEMAN

ONE LUCKY DUCK

Gourmet Vegetarian, Juice Bar
125 E. 17th St. (Irving & 3rd Ave.)
④ ⑤ ⑥ Ⓛ Ⓝ Ⓠ Ⓡ
212 477-7151
Daily 9am–11pm

75 9th Ave. (@ Chelsea Market)
① ② ③ Ⓐ Ⓒ Ⓔ Ⓕ Ⓜ Ⓛ
212 255-4300
Mon–Sat: 10am–9pm,
Sun: 10am–8pm
oneluckyduck.com

Whether it's Ethan Hawke perched on the steps of a café or John Leguizamo emerging from the chill environs of One Lucky Duck toting a Bunny Brew—a raw juice loaded with carrot, apple and ginger—Irving Place is becoming known for its celeb sightings. And if you pick an oddball time—we hit Takeaway at 2:30 on a weekday and snagged a small table amid the colorful pillows—the odds of great people-watching tilt in your favor.

At this tiny outpost of beloved neighboring Pure Food and Wine, all the raw, vegan fare is concocted below 118 degrees, satisfying purists, and many goods are gluten- and nut-free. Savory food proved very tasty; tortilla wraps were malleable and tender, unlike at many similar restaurants, and topped with a sweet sundried tomato spread, smooth cashew cream and a sprightly citrus-tinged guacamole. This, paired with a towering sea vegetable salad of wakame, arame and beets, had us full for hours. Of the freshly extracted juices—the eatery boasts a Norwalk Hydraulic Press juicer, which allows for minimal oxidization of healthy nutrients—we liked the "Thai Green," a savory elixir loaded with pineapple, cilantro and lime. A mango-raspberry smoothie likewise had that eye-opening freshness one expects when paying what are admittedly slightly high prices. But if there's one thing worth paying a premium for here, it's sweets: Pure Food and Wine puts almost every other restaurant we sampled to shame with its naturally-sweetened treats. A faux-mallomar comprised of a pillow of cashew cream, a sprinkle of cocoa and a nutty, earthy base would trick any sugar hound, and a chocolate ganache tart was smoothly, effortlessly decadent. Though I might skip an overly cashew-y take on an Oreo, I'll be back for that mallomar. The sugar-free life never tasted so good.　**ALEX VAN BUREN**

What do you call a polished all-organic eatery? Why, Organika, of course. This Italian-leaning West Village outpost from restaurateur Marcello Assante (Boom, Porta Toscana, Bacco) and executive chef Melissa Muller (previously at Gallo Nero), offers organic wines with pretty decent food to complement

ORGANIKA
Italian
89 Seventh Ave.
(Bleecker St. and Grove St.)
212 414-1900
organikanyc.com
Mon: 5pm–12am,
Tue–Sun: 11am–12am

them. The slightly cramped triangular space is dominated by a marble-topped mahogany bar and an attractive waitstaff that's eager to please. Heavenly smells waft from the open kitchen, so you'll know just when your wild mushroom, arugula, and truffle oil pizza is ready.

The menu is full of simple Mediterranean fare broken down into antipasti, bruschetta, salads, pizza, and pastas, with a roster of daily entrees inspired by the season. Many options are veggie-friendly and even a few are vegan-able, though not intending to be. The plentiful salads are full of crisp garden produce and could stand in for an entrée, though the "Fresca" salad we tried was seriously underdressed. The pizza is also passable, but it is the pasta that solicited low moans from our table. Tiny grass-fed meatballs knocked the rigatoni out of the park. Grilled lamb chops were fork tender and so delicious they had us gnawing on the bones for every last morsel. Though there aren't many dark leafy vegetables, the kitchen did whip up a nice dish of buttery green beans spiked with tarragon.

All of the ingredients on the menu are organic, local, or imported from artisanal producers (like the golden Umbrian olive oil that lines the counter). And just in case you doubt the origin of the prosciutto or capers, you can double check their qualifications on the Food Product Origin card at the back of the menu.　　SCARLETT LINDEMAN

ORGANIQUE
American, Fast Food, Deli
110 E. 23rd St. (Lexington Ave. &
Park Ave. South) ⑥ ⓡ
212 674-2229
organiqueonline.com
Mon–Thu: 7am–10pm,
Fri: 7am–8pm,
Sat: 8am–8pm,
Sun: 10am–8pm

Of the multitude of midtown delis, it's pretty swell to find one that—amid the chemical-filled, fly-dotted buffet bars—offers clean, organic produce and meats for only a dollar or two more. Organique is one such place. The slim space is set up like a typical New York deli, though it seems less crowded than most. Modern decor includes a handful of white plastic tables and a few chairs lining the walls, and it's a fine place to pick up lunch "to go" or an organic cup of joe in the morning.

True to its name, Organique boasts organic produce whenever possible—and labels those items on three large menus that hover over the salad bar. Of the all-organic meats, we quite liked the turkey, moist slabs of which were available by the pound, and wild salmon flecked with dill. (Get there on the early end of the lunch rush—the fish tends to dry out on the heated buffet tins!) Skip not-so-fresh sushi and slightly dry burgers and instead take advantage of the salad bar, with dressings like agave-sweetened miso, or some of the delicious roast vegetable options, which seem to be the kitchen's forte. Baked canoes of deep-orange sweet potatoes came dotted with plump cranberries, and a twist on ratatouille, a mélange of roast eggplant and tomatoes, was melt-in-your-mouth tasty and a nice homage to the late summer season. So though we noted a few places to improve (only iodized salt was available), we were also pleased by touches like filtered water, organic milk for coffee and the locally made 5 Boroughs ice cream available up front. Though it won't be winning awards for Best Manhattan Deli any time soon, choosing smartly among the menu items can yield some surprisingly tasty results, and is a smarter choice than similarly priced neighboring fast-food joints.   ALEX VAN BUREN

Not much beats Otto when it comes to high-end pizza, antipasti, small vegetable plates, and pasta. All are meant to be eaten family-style in the cavernous space smack in the middle of NYU territory on 5th Avenue and 8th Street. With its gently priced dishes, eating at Otto can be a frequent, consistently delicious addition to your restaurant rotation.

OTTO ENOTECA PIZZERIA
Italian, Pizzeria
1 Fifth Ave. (@ 8th St.)
④ ⑤ ⑥ Ⓐ Ⓒ Ⓔ Ⓑ Ⓓ Ⓕ Ⓜ Ⓠ Ⓡ
212 995-9559
ottopizzeria.com
Daily: 11:30am–12am

Like the best Italian trattorias, Otto combines simple ingredients to create flavors and textures that contrast each other, like crunchy cucumber and chewy faro, sweet summer squash with pungent pecorino or bitter broccoli raab tamed with mild ricotta. As always at Mario Batali outposts, the pastas are great, especially when they feature a kick from chili flakes (which is not uncommon from this kitchen).

The pizza is perhaps the best thing at Otto; they are served Roman-style with pies often spilling over the edge of the plates. The combinations here are less successful when they pile too many ingredients on the deliciously flimsy pies, but the margherita with tangy tomato sauce delivers every time. When they have their roasted egg with truffle pizza as a special, snatch it up as it will be the best thing you eat for days—but plan accordingly; it is so rich you might spoil your appetite for quite a while.

Otto is one of the few excellent and affordable restaurants in Manhattan that satisfies a wide-ranging audience. They are happily open til midnight every night, and sustainably-minded guests will be pleased to hear that Otto composts their food waste and even uses recycled cardboard for their pizza boxes. With diverse menu options and impeccable preparations, foodies and casual diners alike will be easily delighted by Otto's Italian family-style dining.   TALIA BERMAN

PEACEFOOD CAFÉ

Gourmet Vegan
460 Amsterdam Ave. (@ 82nd St.)
① Ⓑ Ⓒ
212 362-2266
Daily: 10am–10pm

41 E. 11th St. (@ University Pl.)
④ ⑤ ⑥ Ⓝ Ⓠ Ⓡ Ⓛ
212 979-2288
Daily: 10am–10pm
peacefoodcafe.com

"Now this is vegan food I can get behind," I said, while chewing through a mouthful of cheese-free pizza, packed with broccoli and zucchini. The UWS café serves up gourmet vegan food and delectable pastries. Inside, new moms sip gingery celery juices near pierced punk rockers sampling cashew cheese paninis. Potted plants and stacks of cookbooks lend a casual air and the cuisine, whole foods full of creative twists and bright flavors, happily doesn't rely on mock-meat or deep-frying.

Salads, soups, sandwiches, and pizzas are the bedrocks of the menu. Order side dishes like appetizers; Shanghai-style dumplings filled with chives and mushrooms and vegetable tamales are perfect to share. Chickpea fries release a molten wave of creamy, herb-flecked puree when you bite into the crisp crust. The Asian salad was especially good—a heaping pile of greens, baby Asian vegetables, tomatoes, sprouts, and baked tempeh with sesame vinaigrette had us fighting for the last bite.

Peacefood sources seasonal produce from local suppliers and orders organic ingredients whenever possible. Most soy products, like the milk and bean curd are organic, but the spreadable tofu cheese on some of the sandwiches is not.

Save space for dessert; a dizzying array of all organic scones, cookies, "cheesecakes," and brownies are baked with unbleached white flour (there are spelt and gluten-free options) but without dairy, eggs, or refined sugar. Most selections do contain concentrated cane juice but a couple, like the raw key-lime pie, chocolate ganache, and lemon vanilla cakes use maple syrup and agave nectar to sweeten the deal. Don't pass up the latter—it's so moist and rich you won't believe it's vegan.

SCARLETT LINDEMAN

A number of West Village restaurants clamor for the title of "romantic date place." This eatery tries really, really hard, with superlatively rustic touches that include wide, flat stones on the walls, a fake fireplace, and two terraces illuminated by tiny lights. For the most part, the schtick works.

THE PLACE
New American
310 W. 4th St. (Bank & 12th St.)
① ② ③ Ⓛ Ⓐ Ⓒ Ⓔ Ⓕ Ⓜ PATH
212 924-2711
theplaceny.com
Mon–Fri: 5pm–close,
Sat–Sun: 10:30am–4pm, 5pm–close

And when the fare is all-organic right down to the fluffy bread served before dinner—and it's this good—we have few complaints (though we admit we wish filtered water and organic wines were on offer).

The food is "new American," with nods to France (hello, butter sauces!) and Italy (made-on-the-premises pasta). Start with duck pappardelle; though the slim, wide noodles were a little wobbly for our taste, shreds of organic duck confit—served ragout-style in a sweet tomato sauce with artichoke hearts under a powder of parmigiano reggiano—made this more successful than its pasta counterpart of four teeny squash ravioli overwhelmed by a brown butter sauce. Entrées are what shine here, and happily, they're plated with oodles of vegetables. A bright slash of grilled wild salmon sits smugly on a bed of tender-but-crunchy spears of asparagus and jewel-hued beets. Butter makes an encore in the white wine-spiked sauce pooling under the succulent, fork-tender fish. Leg of lamb was nearly as good, and would especially please those who find lamb a bit "gamy"—the *jus* adds a dark, rich, almost soylike flavor, and gives a savory charge to both tender slices of the beast and a mélange of sautéed summer squash and spinach. Aside from the veggie-packed plates, Jared was pleased by the presence of flat parsley in several dishes, as it's packed with iron and vitamins. Since this chef doesn't overwhelm his plates with it, seeming to know the herb's proper, er, Place, a foodie would hold her protests.

ALEX VAN BUREN

PRET A MANGER
American, British, Fast Food
Multiple Locations (see website)
pret.com

This simple, organic and locally focused soup and sandwich chain is an English import, and it ably contradicts any lingering misapprehensions about the caliber of that country's food.

Instead of potato-based or greasy fare, the charming shops—typically chock-full of tiny tables, a few maroon banquettes, and feather-printed wallpaper—proffer sandwiches, soups, cakes, cookies, muffins, juice and coffees. The 42nd Street location, one of over a dozen citywide, is usually packed with Gothamites seeking a slim, tea-style sandwich stuffed with plush avocado and organic Bell & Evans chicken, or one of several usually tasty soups, like a luscious seasonal puréed butternut squash number. Salads here are often a success, especially a tender salmon and green bean version.

Pret—as the locals call it for short—also succeeds in the beverage arena: Fair-trade, organic coffee is very good, and since beans are rotated (and composted) every two weeks, that cup of joe has an especially fresh kick to it—hard to find in midtown in the morning! The organic milk offered alongside is a swell bonus. If you require something cooler to sip, snag a green tea sweetened with mango or any one of a few sugar-free smoothies. At the 42nd Street location, Bryant Park is just across the street and makes for a fine place to unwind over one of these elixirs or a sweet blueberry-and-pomegranate yogurt drink.

Though tiny healthy touches—sea salt instead of iodized salt, for example—are still missing, this is a fine eatery to snag a quick lunch to go or to stay. Everything's made fresh daily, and leftover sandwiches are donated to charity. This, alongside the fact that most food containers are as biodegradable as possible, will make most diners feel good about their meal as they head back to work.   ALEX VAN BUREN

The only reasonable explanation for Print's under-the-radar status is its far west location. The farm-to-table hotel restaurant may be a harrowing hike from the nearest Hell's Kitchen subway station, but the menu's goat cheese gnocchi alone is worth the walk. The dish's rich, salty ingredients (crispy pancetta and the puffy, cheese-laden capsules) as well as its nutritious produce (fresh corn kernels, string beans, and spinach) create a balanced, well-rounded combination of winter comfort food

PRINT RESTAURANT
New American
653 Eleventh Ave. (@ 48th St.) C E
212 757-2224
printrestaurant.com
Mon-Thu: 7am-10:45am,
   12pm-2:30pm, 5:30pm-10:30pm,
Fri: 7am-10:45am, 12pm-2:30pm,
   5:30pm-11pm,
Sat: 7am-10:45am, 11:30am-3pm,
   5:30pm-11pm,
Sun: 7am-10:45am, 11:30am-3pm,
   5:30pm-9:45pm

and lighter, refreshing summer fare. The heirloom tomato and roasted red pepper soup is also reason enough to head toward the 11th Avenue boondocks. Among the summer's boon of chilled purees and gazpachos, this warm, creamy response is a true standout.

$$$

   Print's entrees effectively integrate local, organic veggie sides and hormone and antibiotic-free proteins. Exhibit A: the duck, whose flavorful jus melds with translucent kohlrabi rectangles and a holiday-colored bed of greens with juicy red berries. Similarly, a red snapper dish creatively invokes the flavors of a fresh bowl of New England clam chowder—the fish, though ours was slightly overcooked, sits atop a cream-infused mixture of corn and parsley. If Print's hushed, undiscovered vibe weren't so appealing, I'd be inclined to shamelessly profess my enthusiasm for its delicious locally-sourced food from Press, Ink 48's scenic rooftop lounge (where the food and panoramic view can be enjoyed). The restaurant is modestly tucked inside Ink48's lobby, its dining room pairing an intricate, psychedelic floor pattern with neutral tables and accents. You don't need to be a hotel guest to enjoy this place before it gets too popular; just duck past the reception desk and run straight to Print's quiet, still-unassuming dining room.

ALLIX GENESLAW

159

PURE FOOD AND WINE
Gourmet Vegan, Raw
54 Irving Pl. (17th & 18th St.)
④ ⑤ ⑥ Ⓛ Ⓝ Ⓠ Ⓡ
212 477-1010
purefoodandwine.com
Daily: 12pm–4pm, 5:30pm–11pm

There's no other way to say it: Pure Food and Wine sexes up raw food. With its red velvet seats, made-for-seduction low lighting, and a romantic garden a nattily-dressed older gentleman one table over described as "to die for," owner Sarma Melngailis's posh Union Square area restaurant is a tribute to gussied-up, uncooked food.

This doesn't mean that for two folks largely accustomed to seeing their food—well, cooked—a noodle-less lasagna isn't going to be a bit of a shock. But the setting makes it all go down easy, and we were impressed by a few inventive twists on classics. Of the starters, a seasonal salad of watermelon—two thick bars of the rosy fruit sandwiching a tangle of baby arugula, a scatter-shot dose of toasted pistachios and a punch of coarse pepper—impressed with over-the-top freshness. Less successful was a faux-ravioli appetizer; limp "noodles" stuffed with cashew filling tasted vaguely peanut-buttery. The kitchen finds its stride in the entrées. Lasagna comprised of thin slices of zucchini, a sweet sundried tomato sauce and a persuasively creamy pine nut cheese was tasty and pretty, to boot. A main course of zucchini blossoms stuffed with cashew cheese in a possum-like imitation of mozzarella, arrived on a bright bed of soft avocado pyramids and sparklingly fresh grape tomatoes.

Please do not skip dessert: It's mandatory to order whatever dairy-free ice cream is on offer, whether it's cardamon-lime, in which the intense herb is beautifully mellowed, or a brilliant, towering V of an ice cream sundae, packed with globes of bright mint ice cream and logs of dense, toothsome chocolate. All ice cream is naturally sweetened and dairy-free, and boy is it brilliant. So snag a glass of organic or biodynamic wine, and hang out in that garden with a friend over that sundae. There are worse ways to spend an evening. ALEX VAN BUREN

Many of us are under the impression that whole wheat pasta is always going to be second-best—that it's one of those compromises we must force ourselves to like. For my part, I'd always put down a fork-swirled bite complaining about the excessive wheatiness of the noodle.

I saw the light, however, in the fairytale-esque garden of Quartino Bottega Organica, an unassuming little Bleecker Street eatery. Here, the whole-wheat, organic pasta is made on the premises and served with, on one occasion, meltingly tender baby artichoke hearts and a dusting of parmigiano reggiano. And if there's a better way to recover from a grueling day of Nolita shopping, I'm not sure what that might be. In addition to said pasta, the menu also has several vegan options. Though we didn't adore our "risotto"—brown rice flecked with basil and tomato—we quite liked gnocchi in a simple, sweet tomato-basil sauce. Pescatarians, take heed: There's no beef or chicken here, but there is always a fish of the day, simply treated (usually grilled or baked). The menu is trim but well curated: foccacia, whole wheat pizza, veggie sides like an excellent baked spinach, and—this had our nutritionist smiling—a brunch menu chock-full of local organic eggs, which can be hard to come by in this part of town. Wine drinkers should know that there are plenty of organic vinos available. With an interior decked out with copper accents and pretty, dim round lights, Quartino Bottega Organica would be an ideal date spot—in or out of the garden.

ALEX VAN BUREN

QUARTINO BOTTEGA ORGANICA
Italian, Gourmet Vegetarian
11 Bleecker St. (Bowery & Lafayette St.) ⑥ Ⓑ Ⓓ Ⓕ Ⓜ
212 529-5133
quartino.com
Mon–Wed: 12pm–11pm,
Th–Sat: 12pm–11:30pm,
Sun: 11pm–10am
Cash only

RIVERPARK

450 East 29th Street
(1st Ave and FDR Dr.) 6
212 729-9790
riverparknyc.com
Mon–Thu: 12pm–10pm,
Fri: 12pm–11pm,
Sat: 11am–11pm,
Sun: 11am–10pm

While many Manhattan restaurants resort to sourcing produce from area farms or scouring greenmarkets for their weekly bounty, Riverpark is taking the farm-to-table concept to another level. Tom Colicchio's modern eatery churns out seasonal specialties boasting ingredients directly from their expansive on-site vegetable garden.

Walk as far east as you can on 29th Street to find this sleek waterfront venue and adjacent urban farm, a lush green rarity in the concrete jungle. If the weather is on your side, settle into the spacious outdoor terrace overlooking the East River. Though a bit noisy from FDR traffic, the serenity of water views make for a pleasant al fresco experience.

Chef Sisha Ortuzar mans the kitchen, producing oft-changing menus of internationally influenced American dishes. At lunch there is a two and three course prix-fixe which includes appetizers, pastas and mains with additional a la carte options and seasonal sides available.

Sweet corn panna cotta adorned with corn-jalapeño salad, avocado, cilantro and creamy huitlacoche vinaigrette was a vibrant starter. The reginetti was a fantastic whole wheat pasta, though the green pepper-spiced sauce with smoked lamb fell a bit short. If they're available, don't miss the fried green tomatoes: perfectly crisped rounds covered in zesty marinara with velvety burrata and fresh basil.

Locally-caught seafood and antibiotic/hormone-free meats are showcased as entrées. The Mediterranean-style lamb burger was a standout: tender meat layered with sharp pecorino, kale slaw and roasted tomato on a toasted English muffin alongside garlicky fries and tzatziki. With high texture complexity, whole Mayan prawns over corn purée, thick bacon lardons, heirloom tomatoes and roasted mushrooms was another meal highlight.

With water views, fresh fare and the award-winning Riverpark Farm, this Kips Bay destination offers a touch of solace from city life.

MEGAN MURPHY

Stringed lights and giant lanterns hang from lofty ceilings, plants creep up to the rooftop farm, and windowed walls open to the street. Rosemary's Enoteca & Trattoria's al fresco feel makes the crowds—who pack the place from door to bar even on a Monday—bearable.

The restaurant is no twin to Bobo, its subterranean French sister, but they share the same roots: fresh, seasonal food sourced close to their West Village homes (for Rosemary's, sometimes at home).

ROSEMARY'S ENOTECA & TRATTORIA
Italian, Wine Bar
18 Greenwich Ave. (@ 10th St.)
Ⓐ Ⓑ Ⓒ Ⓓ Ⓔ Ⓕ Ⓜ ① Ⓛ
212 647-1818
rosemarysnyc.com
Mon–Fri: 8am–4:30pm, 5pm–12am,
Sat–Sun: 10am–4pm, 5pm–12am

Having worked at Babbo and Eataly, Chef Wade Moises knows how to work local ingredients into classic Italian fare. Italian from focacce to finish, Rosemary's food begs to be shared. At the center of the restaurant, an endless communal table makes passing plates feel as natural as it does conversation difficult.

Verdure, like chili-spiced cabbage with pecorino and almonds, eggplant caponata with juicy raisins and cherry tomatoes and colorful beets with hazelnuts and dandelion, packed plenty of flavor into charming little ramekins. The frutti di mare included a refreshing ginger, lemon, jalapeno and mint shrimp. The not-so-chopped chopped salad "Siciliana" was a motley but successful mix: escarole, sliced artichoke, olives, raisins, caper berries, cherry tomatoes, chick peas, ricotta salata and sunflower seeds.

Dive into homemade pastas, like perfectly cooked orecchiette with braised greens and tasty crumbles of homemade sausage. In the "porchettina," pancetta encased a very pink tenderloin, and don't miss the accompanying frutta mostarda and fennel. Charred and tender slices of grilled lamb leg warmed the dish's winning surprise, a heap of pulled lamb stewing beside braised greens. Roasted peaches and creamy sheep's milk ricotta sealed the deal, though there were too few peaches.

The servers are well meaning, if spotty, but they'll grow into the hustle soon enough. As long as Rosemary's keeps bringing the food from rooftop to table, the crowds will keep coming.   JACLYN EINIS

ROUGE TOMATE
New American
10 E. 60th St.
(5th & Madison Ave.)
④ ⑤ ⑥ Ⓡ Ⓕ
646-237-8977
rougetomatenyc.com
Mon–Sat: 12pm–3pm,
  5:30pm–10:30pm

This split-level restaurant feels like the love child of a celebrity spa and a modern art museum, which we suppose shouldn't shock us on the Upper East Side. Sexy two-tone white leather-and-wooden chairs nestle next to pale oak booths and wooden tables, and a plethora of bright-red tchotchkes—light boxes, a pool of cranberries, square candles—had us wondering whether Martha Stewart herself had just stormed through in a Valentine's Day-induced frenzy, leaving a scarlet trail in her wake. No matter. The food here is very good and quite healthy: Chef Jeremy Bearman (a Daniel Boulud alum) created a menu approved by an on-staff nutritionist. They hope to marry "well-executed cuisine" to "authentic nutrition." Okay by us!

The first collaboration we tasted, that ho-hum standby squash soup (which was a knockout here) lent a round, beautifully *umami* flavor by an ethereal cloud of licorice foam, with diced apples and pecans delivering a precise textural counterpoint to the silky broth. The second sampling, a fluke tartar stacked with pea shoots, squash, wakame seaweed, and pear slices, was quite good, but rather texturally overwhelming. Entrées were on more solid turf, like a skewer of toothsome venison served with garlicky mint raita and a flurry of pale golden bulgur wheat. Only a chicken entrée took another "kitchen sink" approach to texture, with extremely crunchy chestnuts, soft raisins, tart cherries and fluffy quinoa comprising an oddly chaotic bed for the bird. But that bird was shellacked golden, organic and utterly juicy, so we will admit to splitting hairs. Overall, we were happy, especially given the number of organic wines, the filtered water and the abundance of vegetable options. The icing on the cake? The seductively smooth tables and floors were stamped as eco-friendly by the Forest Stewardship Council—a small triumph of substance over style.   ALEX VAN BUREN

Northwest-born New Yorkers will saunter through the door of this little café and do a double-take: It's a dead ringer for any Portland, Oregon café. And brunch on our visit was—an avowed carnivore winces to type these words of a vegan eatery—fantastic.

SACRED CHOW
Gourmet Vegan
227 Sullivan St.
(Bleecker & W. 3rd St.)
① Ⓐ Ⓒ Ⓔ Ⓑ Ⓓ Ⓕ Ⓜ PATH
212 337-0863
sacredchow.com
See website for hours

The hippie vibe is on the premises in a major way: Gargan-tuan faux-Japanese lanterns dangle overhead; the logo is of a mellow-looking cartoon cow practicing yoga; our waiter was über-friendly despite being the only one working his shift. Cynical Gothamites will have to bite their tongues at the sincerity of it all. But the delicious, 95% organic food will get them talking again. Curried tofu scramble—so egglike we experienced momentary disorientation—was served with a side of addictively smoky new potatoes that count among the best we've eaten at brunch. Spying a waffle made with spelt and oats, we ordered it and braced ourselves (spelt, though healthy, is tricky to make tasty) only to be wowed by its plushness. If I'd still been on the fence, a tiny pitcher of sweet, fresh blueberry sauce swimming with berries would have won me over. Even a side of curry-flecked steamed broccoli, and a savory tempeh reuben topped with perfectly golden, sweet caramelized onions impressed us.

Those with dietary restrictions will be pleased to see that every dish is labeled gluten-, wheat-, or sugar-free, so they can order without interrogating the waiter. Such a thing is a concern on a date, a vibe this spot also has in spades, with cushy seats by a sunny window looking like prime romantic turf. On evening outings, those who wish to can tipple on local beers like Ommegang or kosher (the place is certified), organic wines. With such abundant options, and service so gallant—our waiter dropped a stack of plates, but walked away still smiling broadly—all can seem quite right with the world.   ALEX VAN BUREN

SAUCE

Italian

78 Rivington St. (Orchard & Allen St.)

Ⓕ Ⓙ Ⓜ

212 420-7700

saucerestaurant.com

Mon–Thu: 5pm–12am,

Fri–Sat: 11am–1am,

Sun: 11am–12am

The latest in Chef Frank Prisinzano's nascent east side empire, Sauce replicates the simple equation that keeps his three other restaurants crowded: affordable, Nonna-inspired Italian in an intimate yet group-friendly atmosphere. An unstuffy, casual attitude compliments a serious approach to ingredients. Heritage Farms meats are butchered in-house and in plain view of Rivington Street passersby, making Sauce a happy place for carnivores. And while we were too late to snag that day's bollito misto, a mixed plate of braised meats, we relished in fresh, flavorful grass-fed beef meatballs over Pugliese bread soaked in gravy (e.g. tomato sauce) from the menu's "ragu by the piece" section.

We enjoyed more of that tender meat in the elegantly plated—or rather, planked—polenta plate, prepared for two or more. The rich, soft polenta poured on wood and topped with bolognese, olive oil, and parmesan, "the plank" is pure spoonable, buttery bliss. While the above are not for the salt-averse, some dishes, like the kale and potato gnocchi, are best reserved for the salt-smitten. Nevertheless, we were willing to take an extra glass of Montepulciano to keep nibbling at the perfectly dense, handmade dumplings in "Dad's marinara."

More balanced was the mouth-watering roasted red pepper stuffed with farro, mushroom, and sage. Capped with bubbling parmesan, it was a comforting, tender start to the meal. Order it alongside one (or several) salads. Though tempted by a "stacked" salad with bitter greens, coarse black salt, and beefsteak tomatoes, we opted for a refreshing medley of crisp escarole, ricotta salata, mint leaves, castelvetrano olives, and pine nuts. Beautifully, lightly seasoned with lemon and olive oil, it was tasty enough to warrant a prompt return or perhaps even a solo trip to the welcoming bar.   JACLYN EINIS

Father-daughter duo Tony and Marisa May have revamped San Domenico (the late Madison Square Park inhabitant) into SD26, a younger, sleeker space with a numerical nod to its new location. Giant, multicolored lint balls hang from the high ceiling as if spun mid-air by mutant arachnids; red walls and black recessed booths and intimate two-seaters furnish the otherwise colorless dining room. Hip iPad wine lists on each table

SD26
Italian
19 E. 26th St. (5th Ave. & Madison Ave.)
④ ⑤ ⑥ Ⓝ Ⓒ Ⓡ Ⓕ Ⓜ Ⓛ
212 265-5959
sd26ny.com
Mon–Th: 11:30am–2:30pm,
   5:30pm–11pm,
Fri: 11:30am–2:30pm,
   5:30pm–11:30pm,
Sat: 5:30pm–11:30pm,
Sun: 5pm–10pm

are more presumptuous than utilitarian, their daunting magnitude causing them to function as clunky centerpieces rather than navigable digital sommeliers.

The menu, though not quite as lofty as its computerized counterpart, is also fairly ambitious—salumeria and formaggeria sections initiate, followed by vegetable, pasta, fish, and meat chapters. I feared the food would emulate the decor's purported trendiness with gelees and foams galore, but luckily it tends to veer toward the traditional side. The only vague approximation of molecular gastronomy is a welcome lighter-than-air puff of ricotta and parmesan cheese which arrives as an addictive dip for the chilled eggplant and tomato terrine. Also crave-inducing is the parsley sauce that accompanies the assorted grilled vegetables; their flavor is elevated by the greenish condiment. Potato and leek ravioli is a creative rendition of the filled pasta, though the bland middles, overcooked exteriors, and soupy pesto topping were a little trying. Go for the braised beef cheeks instead—their tender texture deems a knife superfluous, while the polenta provides a creamy, jus-absorbing reinforcement. SD26 may feel a little hokey and contrived at times, but its tasty dishes and endearingly old-school waiters (who pronounced even the make of my phone, "Black-a-Berry", in a sing-songy intonation) are what stuck with us.   ALLIX GENESLAW

SOUEN

Asian, Macrobiotic

28 E. 13th St. (University & 5th Ave.)

①②③④⑤⑥ⓁⓃⓆⓇ

212 627-7150

Mon–Sat: 11am–10:30pm,
Sun: 11am–10pm

210 Sixth Ave. (@ Prince St.)

①ⒶⒸⒺⒷⒹⒻⓂ

212 807-7421

Mon–Fri: 11:30am–10:30pm,
Sat: 11am–10:30pm,
Sun: 11am–10pm
souen.net

Stepping into Souen is like discovering a tiny slice of California on a strip of 13th street teeming with NYU co-eds. The first thing to notice is a veritable wall of plants: Leafy greens line the woodsy, open-air terrace as well as the bustling second floor. Souen is a popular spot for work meetings as well as for students, and it's fairly mellow. It is also one of the standbys Jared recommends to clients, since everything is organic, dark greens are plentiful and desserts are naturally sweetened. Even diners who flip when they see the word "macrobiotic" on the menu will remain calm here: Seafood and sushi options are abundant, so there truly is something for everyone.

The absence of refined sugar—and even salts—becomes a comfort when digging into the uniformly clean-tasting food. Though a few dishes seemed a little lacking at first, such as the boiled-and-steamed veggies that accompanied our entrées, my palate largely adjusted to the under-salting over the course of the meal. Sure, I would have loved to douse a few things with salt, such as a pile of unappealing yams, but a creamy carrot dressing nicely balanced steamed kale, and my tuna steak speckled with white-and-black sesame seeds came with sweet, caramelized edges. Wild salmon was even better, encrusted in an otherworldly bright-red beet coating. Even our sole sushi roll was a pleasant surprise: Beautifully crisp softshell crab arrived bundled in nori with purple seaweed, avocado, cucumbers and asparagus. When Jared calls this high-energy food, I can't disagree. I was full—surprisingly so—for the rest of the day, despite having eaten very little.

ALEX VAN BUREN

The macrobiotic style of eating (based on whole grains, legumes, and leafy, root, and sea vegetables) is often associated with tired cafeterias serving plate after plate of brown rice. Not so with Souen Organic Ramen. The space is easy on the eyes—small and narrow, flanked by a long cream booth with pale wood accents.

SOUEN EAST VILLAGE
Asian, Macrobiotic
326 E 6th St. (1st Ave. & 2nd Ave.) **F** **L**
212 388-1155
souen.net
Mon–Sat: 12pm–11:30pm,
Sun: 12pm–10pm

More stylish bistro than hippie co-op, Souen Ramen is an offshoot of the pre-existing Souen establishments. The focus is, of course, ramen, but steaming bowls of broth and noodles swap the usual meaty accompaniments for delicate miso and carrots.

Souen's ramen bathes in silky soups with a choice of soba, udon, or rice noodles. The "Mucho Vege Miso Ramen" we tried relaxed in a rich miso broth with squash and broccoli. Jared liked the velvety texture, but I yearned for a slice of pork belly. Fish is the only animal product on offer, and on our last visit, a piece of perfectly cooked, buttery halibut graced our meal.

The non-ramen items are also winners: a lightly cooked kale side was supple and perfumed with garlic; the burdock kimpira, a wok-fried mixture of carrot, lotus root, and burdock sings with sesame; the cold ramen salad is refreshingly vinegary with slivered veggies; and a sprightly seaweed salad was gorgeous in both presentation and taste. I liked the slightly sweet iced apple lemon KukiCha Tea while Jared preferred the grain coffee: a toasty substitute made with organic barley and rye that can wean caffeine addicts.

Desserts—like the chocolate creamy parfait and the fruit kanten—are sugar, egg, dairy, and wheat free, and are naturally sweetened with maple syrup. With seaweed, piles of veggies, and no sugar in sight, macrobiotic restaurants are easy champions in the realm of health. Fortunately, Souen Ramen packs in the flavor too.

SCARLETT LINDEMAN

SPRING NATURAL KITCHEN

New American

474 Columbus Ave. (@ 83rd St.) Ⓑ Ⓒ ❶
646 596-7434
springnaturalkitchen.com
Mon–Tue: 11:30am–5pm, 5:30pm–10:30pm,
Wed–Thu: 11:30am–5pm, 5:30pm–11:30pm,
Fri: 11:30am–5pm, 5:30pm–12:30am,
Sat: 10:30am–4:30pm, 5:30pm–12:30am,
Sun: 10:30am–4:30pm, 5:30pm–10:30pm

The open and airy Spring Natural Kitchen is a welcome and much-needed addition to the Upper West Side's healthy restaurant selection. Brick walls, dark wooden floors and matching ceilings invoke an upscale diner with fresh flowers and cozy candlelight to boot. Serving seasonal foods with vegan and vegetarian options alongside grass-fed, free-range meat, the conscious and extensive menu also features clearly labeled gluten-free dishes.

Our meal began with four meaty baby back ribs that just fell off the bone slathered in a thick, dark plum cacao sauce. The perfectly balanced sauce ranged from sweet to bitter and had none of the chalkiness that cacao sauces often do. The roasted beet salad featured crispy shallots, baby spinach, pickled sun-dried cherries, Moroccan-spiced goat cheese with a white balsamic-hazelnut vinaigrette. The cherries were deliciously sweet and chewy, but the cheese was too heavily spiced. The ingredients were tasty and wholesome, but the excess of cheese and extensive mix of ingredients left our palates overwhelmed.

While the stir-fry organic vegetables with tempeh over organic brown rice and tamari-garlic-ginger sauce was a substantial dish, it was bland and begged for some hot sauce. We wish we'd opted for the curry.

The roasted organic salmon was a refreshingly vibrant and welcome course. Pomelo, navel orange, fennel, red radish, roasted red bliss potatoes and a tart-yet-sweet tamarind-honey glaze provided a colorful bed for the salmon. The grilled natural grass-fed angus beef burger satisfied our cravings: a juicy patty topped with sautéed mushrooms, grilled red onions, and melted cheese all on a toasted sesame bun with hand-cut french fries.

However they serve it, Spring Natural Kitchen offers a range of dishes catered to specific diets, making it easy for omnivores and vegans alike to relish in good ingredients and hearty flavors.   **AMY SUNG**

Spring Street Natural is in the heart of SoHo, and feels like it: Men in skinny jeans waltz through the doors and keep their sunglasses on for the duration of brunch; hungover couples slump awaiting electrolyte delivery at bright window tables; bubbly families happily ignore them both. The eatery is designed for function, though it's pretty enough during the day, with soaring windows on all sides letting the sun shine in. Otherwise, it has a somewhat chaotic suburban

SPRING STREET NATURAL
New American
62 Spring St. (@ Lafayette St.)
⑥ Ⓑ Ⓓ Ⓕ Ⓜ Ⓡ
212 966-0290
springstreetnatural.com
Mon–Th: 9am–11:30pm,
Fri: 9am–12:30am,
Sat: 10:30am–12:30am,
Sun: 10:30am–11:30pm

feel: Green leather-covered chairs park at wooden tables placed close together, with only a few booths for the lucky.

That said, we still like it for a midday fix of American cuisine with several vegan and vegetarian options. We swung by for brunch, when it's perhaps the most packed; sidewalk tables are stuffed with customers spying on their fellow SoHo shoppers when the weather is mild. Grub is typically solid, such as a side of garlicky sautéed spinach spritzed with lemon, and the many organic meats include a few toothsome chicken sausages (paired with maple syrup for a guilty fix). We do wish the owners would attend to a few more health-oriented details—filtered water, organic milk, non-refined sugar—so feel free to give feedback (a chef told us "customers haven't demanded organic milk yet"—hint, hint!) But tasty good-for-you foods can be found here, including organic eggs and a tower of tempeh for the snack-craving vegan—three fried sticks of protein balancing in a pool of spicy tomato and green cilantro sauces. A grass-fed New York strip steak sandwich was also pretty good, plated on toasted ciabatta with a tangle of mixed greens and a smear of lime-chile mayonnaise. Restaurants pay attention to feedback, so feel free to chat with your waiter, and perhaps help Spring Street Natural get even more Natural.   ALEX VAN BUREN

THE STANDARD GRILL

New American

848 Washington St. (@13th St.)

Ⓐ Ⓒ Ⓔ Ⓛ ① ② ③

212 645-4100

thestandardgrill.com

Mon–Thu: 7am–4pm, 5:30pm–12am,
Fri: 7am–4pm, 5:30pm–1am,
Sat: 11am–4pm, 5:30pm–1am,
Sun: 11am–4pm, 5:30pm–12am

Tucked under the West Side's ever expanding High Line, the flagship restaurant of André Balazs's Standard Hotel is a novel addition to the trendy Meatpacking District. In a neighborhood renowned for a bevy of pretentious hotspots, The Standard Grill sets a new dining standard with its sophisticated, laid-back atmosphere and exceptionally friendly service. This sprawling contemporary eatery boasts an outdoor terrace, sun-drenched front lounge and airy main

\$ \$

dining room filled with white clothed tables, tufted leather banquettes and a floor embedded with thousands of copper pennies.

With a heavy emphasis on market fresh ingredients, executive chef Dan Silverman presents a seasonal menu of refined and updated classic American fare. We enjoyed a salad of crisp Satur Farm baby romaine lightly coated with lemon garlic vinaigrette and crested with succulent briny anchovies, but the appetizer knockout was a silken chilled carrot soup—the cool, cardamom-laced purée swirled with creamy orange-maple yogurt invited me to lap up every last drop. Each elegantly presented entrée was delightful, including a flaky Atlantic striped bass over a lush pistachio-black truffle sauce and surprisingly refreshing housemade fettuccine ribbons enlivened by citrus, saffron, plump shrimp and fresh spring peas.

A limited offering of vegetarian-friendly options rounds out the menu along with several vegetable accompaniments, like tender broccoli rabe sauteed with spicy garlic-chili bread crumbs. We also noted an impressive raw bar, expertly-crafted cocktails and an extensive list of prominently Italian, French and California wines, though it would've been nice to see an organic offering or two in the mix. Overall, with an inviting ambiance, attentive staff and inspired cuisine, one thing is certain: there's nothing standard about this grill.   MEGAN MURPHY

Manhattan's latest salad-showcasing eatery has landed in the space adjacent to The NoMad Hotel. The first NYC branch of this fast-casual D.C.-based chain (and 20th location on the East Coast), Sweetgreen focuses on sustainably sourcing local and organic

SWEETGREEN
New American, Fast Food
1164 Broadway (27th St. and 28th St.)
(1) (6) (N) (R) (F) (M)
(646) 449-8855
sweetgreen.com
Mon–Sun: 10:30am–11pm

ingredients from area farmers and purveyors.

Sweetgreen's lively interior features tables and rear bleacher seating made from reclaimed wood along with a back wall chalkboard touting the state and specific farms that all seasonal ingredients are derived from. Creative customers can design made-to-order salads and wrap masterpieces with a base of options—warm quinoa and farro grains, shredded kale, chopped romaine, and organic mesclun, arugula, and baby spinach—and an array of proteins, including unique vegetarian options like baked falafel, with add-ins of assorted veggies, fruits, nuts and organic seeds. Or simply choose from several featured combos like the hearty "Guacamole Greens" with tender roasted chicken, creamy avocado, grape tomatoes, red onion, and crushed tortilla chips, topped with lime-cilantro-jalapeno vinaigrette and fresh lime juice.

Heat seekers will relish the kicked up flavors in the "Spicy Sabzi," which layers greens, spicy quinoa and vegetables, sweet basil, sprouts and roasted organic tofu with carrot-chili vinaigrette, finished with a kiss of sriracha. The savory-meets-sweet "Santorini" was a real standout— plump citrus shrimp, tangy feta cheese, red grapes and chickpeas over romaine, all dressed with creamy cucumber-basil yogurt. Takeaway sides and seasonal soups round out the savory menu offerings.

Organic cold-pressed juices in personalities like "purify," "energize" and "detox" provide refreshment, along with an organic frozen yogurt bar. My delicious froyo finish consisted of silky and tart Stonyfield yogurt, plump blueberries, flax seeds and local honey drizzle. With generous portions, high quality produce, and fresh, vibrant flavors, toss Sweetgreen onto your list of go-to salad spots.　　MEGAN MURPHY

TAKASHI
Japanese, Korean
456 Hudson St.
(Morton & Barrow St.)
Ⓐ Ⓒ Ⓔ Ⓑ Ⓓ Ⓕ Ⓜ ① ②
212 414-2929
takashinyc.com
Mon–Thu: 6pm–11pm,
Fri–Sat: 5:30pm–12am,
Sun: 5pm–10:30pm

Despite my best efforts, I am not an offal devotee. I love liver's gamy intensity and agree that sweetbreads taste like delicious chicken nuggets, but I don't yearn for plates of fried veal hearts and steamy pig intestines like many of my contemporaries.

So I cannot say I was itching to go to Takashi, a grill-it-yourself operation in the West Village. But the restaurant is great—especially the beef, which comes from local New York State farms, Pat LaFrieda, and Oregonian Waygu cows courtesy of Japanese Premium Beef.

The meal starts with beef sushi. Try the Gyutoro-Temaki Sushi, ground flap steak formed into perfect squares perched atop sushi rice, adorned with sesame seeds and scallions. The sushi comes with nori for wrapping the sushi as well as soy sauce and fresh wasabi for a swanky and refreshing touch. Speaking of swanky touches, the flash-boiled Achilles-tendon appetizer comes topped with a regal mound of saffron that, while impressive, doesn't ease the crunchy-chewy confrontation that the tendons present.

This is quickly forgotten with the onset of the cook-it-yourself meats. The house-marinated skirt steak yields generous bursts of flavor between the uniquely-textured layers. Beef cheeks are like beef bacon. Sliced thin and shriveled to crispy bites, their flavor is more complex than the other cuts of beef. The short ribs are slightly disappointing; the evenly-distributed marbling results in a slightly chewy bite when grilled on a direct flame. Order the fresh vegetables on the side; delight in the peanutty-miso mayonnaise it arrives with, and use the romaine lettuce and cabbage leaves as snappy wrappers for the rich beef.

Takashi is warm and welcoming. The toilet is self-cleaning. The service at Takashi is thoughtful and genuine, from when the door is opened for you to the slices of Wrigley's gum that appear with your check—one for every diner.   **TALIA BERMAN**

Adjacent to Eli's Manhattan and W.I.N.E. (Eli Zabar's eponymous produce and prepared food market and his wine and spirits shop, respectively), Zabar's Taste showcases simple, quality ingredients that often hail from the owner's very own rooftop. There is nothing fussy about the interior (that is, unless you

TASTE RESTAURANT AND WINE BAR
American
1413 Third Ave. (80th St. & 81st St.)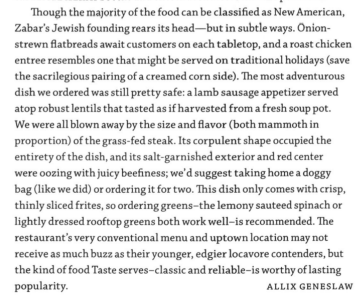
212 717-9798
elizabar.com
Mon–Fri: 7am–3:30pm, 5:30pm–close,
Sat–Sun: 8am–3pm, 5:30pm–close

consider the persnickety ordering practices of some of the seasoned patrons); the glass facade is open to the 3rd Avenue elements, and casual red leather booths and chestnut shutters line the perimeter.

Though the majority of the food can be classified as New American, Zabar's Jewish founding rears its head—but in subtle ways. Onion-strewn flatbreads await customers on each tabletop, and a roast chicken entree resembles one that might be served on traditional holidays (save the sacrilegious pairing of a creamed corn side). The most adventurous dish we ordered was still pretty safe: a lamb sausage appetizer served atop robust lentils that tasted as if harvested from a fresh soup pot. We were all blown away by the size and flavor (both mammoth in proportion) of the grass-fed steak. Its corpulent shape occupied the entirety of the dish, and its salt-garnished exterior and red center were oozing with juicy beefiness; we'd suggest taking home a doggy bag (like we did) or ordering it for two. This dish only comes with crisp, thinly sliced frites, so ordering greens–the lemony sauteed spinach or lightly dressed rooftop greens both work well–is recommended. The restaurant's very conventional menu and uptown location may not receive as much buzz as their younger, edgier locavore contenders, but the kind of food Taste serves–classic and reliable–is worthy of lasting popularity.

ALLIX GENESLAW

TELEPAN

New American

72 W. 69th St. (Columbus Ave. &
Central Park West) ① ② ③ Ⓑ Ⓒ

212 580-4300

telepan-ny.com

Mon: 5pm–10pm,
Tue: 11:30am–2:30pm, 5pm–10:30pm,
Wed–Thu: 11:30am–2:30pm,
    5pm–10:30pm,
Fri: 11:30am–2:30pm, 5pm–11:30pm,
Sat: 11am–2:30pm, 5pm–11:30pm,
Sun: 11am–3pm, 5pm–10:30pm

Sparklingly fresh produce and organic meat are the focus of this relaxed-but-refined UWS eatery, which ably takes up the mantle of locavore-centric downtown forefathers Savoy and Blue Hill. Since the elegant fare here is a little pricey, it's worth choosing your ambiance when making a reservation: On the right, behind a U-shaped, elegant bar, are clusters of cozy banquettes—rather more intimate and suitable to a date. To the left is a more formal dining room, with brighter lighting that emphasizes the light, mint-green walls and Edward Hopper-esque contemporary art.

On both sides, Euro-flecked fare shines. Chef-owner Bill Telepan has worked with such Gallic luminaries as Daniel Boulud at Le Cirque and Gilbert Le Coze at Le Bernadin, and it shows, both in a classic cheese *gougères amuse-bouche* paired with bright, flavorful gazpacho and the hearty, earthy hangar steak glazed in decadent oxtail bone-marrow sauce that ended our meal. Telepan takes the root of his food seriously, sourcing within 250 miles whenever possible.

If it's chilly outside, start with a heartwarming soup. Drifts of bread float amidst pigeon peas, root vegetables and carrots in a simple, parmesan-infused vegetable broth. Move on to an unmissable lobster Bolognese—the lightest twist on that Italian classic imaginable, with chunks of the buttery crustacean swimming in a sweet tomato sauce dotted with fronds of dill. Ironically, we also ordered an entrée of "the poor man's lobster"—monkfish—in a luxurious dill-buttermilk sauce. Though it can't go tail to tail with that lobster, it was just fine—although carnivores will happily ignore all fish items and take up their sharp knives for the aforementioned steak, perhaps the most tender, well-marbled grass-fed beef we encountered. Skip dessert, if you're avoiding sugar: None are naturally sweetened (yet), though with the chef's eggs-to-apples approach to food, we'd be unsurprised to see that around the corner. **ALEX VAN BUREN**

You're in Chelsea, on the go, and hungry. Thankfully there's Terri on 23rd St between 6th and 7th Aves, which aptly bills itself as organic vegetarian cuisine in a hurry (it's actually vegan). Plan accordingly; it's mostly counter service, and seating is limited to a few very slick barstools.

TERRI
Vegan, Fast Food
60 West 23rd St. (5th Ave. & 6th Ave.)
① ② ⑥ Ⓝ Ⓡ
212-647-8810
terrinyc.com
Mon–Fri: 6am–11pm,
Sat–Sun: 8am–9pm

100 Maiden Lane (@ Pearl St.)
② ③ ④ ⑤
212 742-7901
Mon–Fri: 7am–10pm,
Sat–Sun: 10am–9pm

While there are quite a few sandwiches like the Thai chicken wrap that feature soy and wheat protein "chicken", Jared recommends steering clear of the processed protein. I'd have to agree; while the wrap was filled with bountiful julienned vegetables and a peanut sauce, the faux-chicken offering was sadly lacking in expected Thai flavors. Instead, choose options like the portobello chimichurri sandwich, for this is where Terri finds real success with massive infusions of flavor. Grilled portobello and zucchini sandwiched between toasted focaccia with luscious mint pesto had this omnivore satisfied. The spinach salad is sizably portioned with crunchy jicama sticks and tangy hearts of palm (though we wished for more toppings on the heap of greens). Wash it all down with the refreshing ginger lemonade— Terri's housemade version packs a delightful punch of ginger.

If you're craving a naturally sweetened mouthful, grab a smoothie like the creamy Sunset Proposal, a slurry of mango, pineapple, coconut, and soy milk (though Jared was thrilled to see that rice milk is offered in place of soy at no extra charge). You can also opt for the delicious date bar—but be sure to eat the crumbly dessert carefully.

Kosher, vegan, organic, with rice milk and gluten-free bread on demand; Terri is prepared to meet any vegetarian craving. If you stop by on a weather-perfect day, scoop up food at Terri for a picnic at nearby Madison Square Park.   ANDREA LYNN

TERTULIA

Spanish, Tapas

359 6th Ave. (W. 4th St. & Waverly Pl.)

Ⓐ Ⓑ Ⓒ Ⓓ Ⓔ Ⓕ Ⓜ ①

646 559-9909

tertulianyc.com

Mon–Thu: 11:30am–3pm,
     5:30pm–11pm,
Fri: 11:30am–3pm, 5:30pm–12am,
Sat: 11:30am–3:30pm, 5:30pm–12am,
Sun: 11:30am–3:30pm, 5:30pm–11pm

Spanish for "social gathering," Tertulia lives up to its name. On a hot day, the front bar may feel more crowded than social, but stick around. Drink some cider; it's worth the wait.

Seamus Mullen has channeled the spirit of northern Spain's *sidrerías* into a lively West Village gastropub, replete with brick arches, tapped oak barrel and hanging pig's legs. Communal tables fill much of the dining room, where guests can peek into the open kitchen and gaze at food rising and lowering to the perfect temperature in the wood-burning crank oven.

Beyond the platter of cut-to-order Iberico ham, made from acorn-fed, pastured pigs, toasts dominate the starters. Marinated for a nice acidic kick, mushrooms met smoked ricotta and pine nuts on Tostas Setas, while Tostas Mejillones doused grilled mussels and raisins in an addictive mix of fennel jam and *allioli* (garlicky mayonnaise).

Thankfully, Tapas and Sartenes (skillets) are designed to be shared; it's tough to choose just one or two. We started with Cogullos, a lemony gem lettuce salad with asparagus and fried quinoa, the vegan answer to bacon bits. With the help of our waiter, we chose Cocochas al Pil-Pil from a long list of specials. A few bites of the rich, gelatinous cheek of the *merluza* (hake) fish resting in the cooking oil (*al pil-pil*), was just enough. The Arroz a la Plancha folded earthy wild mushrooms, snails and fennel into a toasty roll of creamy Calasparra rice. Topped with crisp slices of fennel and Iberico ham, the rice formed a crunchy layer around a risotto-like center. Scooped up alongside cauliflower and creamy farro, an impossibly tender lamb fell apart with a mere touch of a spoon.

No matter the heat; I'll happily gather by Tertulia's fire any season.

JACLYN EINIS

This vegetarian pizza joint has been turning out pies to East Village denizens and bar-crawlers for a little over a decade now. Most produce is organic and cheese is both kosher and hormone-free, making this a more salubrious slice option than its neighboring competitors. Decor is slightly lacking, with a few chairs strewn about, a couple of unsteady red metal tables, and a spooky, lockless bathroom in the back of the restaurant. So snag your slice "to go" if you're looking for ambiance.

VIVA HERBAL PIZZERIA
Vegetarian, Pizzeria, Fast Food
179 2nd Ave. (11th & 12th St.)
212 420-8801
Mon–Thu: 11am–11:30pm,
Fri–Sat: 11am–12am,
Sun: 11am–11:30pm

The pizza is solid, with an extraordinary variety of crusts on offer that include unbleached white, whole wheat, cornmeal and even spelt. The latter, for those unaccustomed to it, is a red grain that provides a certain earthiness to dough. It's much better for you than whole wheat or white, and at Viva it adds a density of flavor to a simple trio of mozzarella, spinach and tomato toppings. Fans of nearby Two Boots should sample the cornmeal crust, but should avoid the "Mexicali" number unless they can really stand the heat: A bevy of toppings include chopped cilantro, onions, tomatoes and an onslaught of take-no-prisoners jalapeños. I preferred a simple margarita slice—very good on traditional dough, and totally fine on whole wheat—but pizza-topping options are kaleidoscopic, including broccoli, roast peppers and "green tea herbed miso-tofu," so load up on veggie toppings.

Note that this is Gotham we're talking about, and these slices may not win awards among purists. But with vegan options, pesticide-free produce and healthier drinks like naturally sweetened sodas to provide a welcome respite from the typical Coke-slinging pizzeria, this is a wise move for hungry wanderers in a pinch. Call ahead and snag a pie made to order and lug it home or to nearby Thompson Square Park. It'd be very New York of you.   ALEX VAN BUREN

V-NOTE
Gourmet Vegan
1522 1st Ave. (79th & 80th St.) 6
212 249-5009
v-notenyc.com
Sun–Thu: 12pm–4:30pm, 5pm–10pm,
Fri–Sat: 12pm–4:30pm, 5pm–10:30pm

V-Note's Upper East Side location attracts both downtown vegan veterans and curious seniors who made the harrowing walk (or scoot) from up the block. Whether you're bumping elbows with Edna and her track suit entourage or the spring chicken couple, it's refreshing that V-Note's cushioned, dining room-length bench is a welcoming setting for its diverse vegan, vegetarian, and sustainable food fans. Owned by the creator of Blossom and Cafe Blossom, V-Note also offers an impressive all-vegan, all-organic wine and beer list. Rather than merely focusing on veggies, the menu includes a fair amount of soy and gluten proteins as well. Among these dishes is the feijoadinha with smokey tempeh (Jared's protein pick), a southwestern-inspired stew of tempeh, black beans, squash, potatoes, and crisp potato chips. The broth could have been more viscous and robust, though I did enjoy the textural contrast between the tender stewed potatoes and their crunchy, baked counterpart. The two most successful options we tried were those that nixed the protein—the mushroom risotto and roasted pumpkin and sweet potato gnocchi. The creamy, tomato-based risotto expanded my mushroom vocabulary to include varieties like trumpet and lobster. These corpulent species mimicked the weight and feel of protein, while the inclusion of thin seaweed strips invoked the taste of seafood. As for the gnocchi appetizer, the doughy potato orbs' absence of seasoning was rescued by an extremely flavorful sage-infused sauce and a cap of fibrous, garlic-infused kale. I tend to briskly head in the opposite direction when I hear the word "vegan", but V-Note's warm, classic interior, friendly staff, and fearless approach to vegan cooking were a pleasant surprise.

ALLIX GENESLAW

Ah, Whole Foods. Is it a store? A meeting place? A shrine? Whatever it is, the grocery behemoth renowned for its all-natural foods has its fans, and they contribute to the seven Gotham locations feeling like madhouses much of the time.

WHOLE FOODS
New American, Fast Food
Multiple Locations (see website)
wholefoodsmarket.com
Daily: 8am–11pm

It's a boon, then, that each Whole Foods has its own "restaurant," so you can squirrel your finds—whether organic greens, gluten-free cookies or a tasty antibiotic-free chicken soup—back to a table. The Columbus Circle location boasts a cacophonous but fun caféteria and juice bar; the Bowery shop sports a calmer second-level eatery with electrical outlets accessible to laptop-luggers. We swung by the Bowery location, where I love to lurk in the adjacent Beer Room to snag tap suds like upstate's Captain Lawrence Liquid Gold poured into recyclable growlers "to go." If swinging by for a quick bite, the Bowery's faux-"trattoria" offers perfectly serviceable pasta that includes a few wheat noodle numbers and pumpkin ravioli in brown butter sauce flecked with sage. The salad bar almost always boasts a few treasures—at the Columbus Circle spot, organic chicken tikka masala has been the bomb on several occasions—and at the Bowery store, the salad bar was packed with good stuff—lentils here, a super-fresh mixed-green salad there. As per desserts, wheat- and gluten-free options are available in the bakery. Just be sure—no matter which salad, sushi or dessert bar you're at—you read the ingredients listed over each offering. Watch out for sugar! Not so healthy, people. Although if you're going for cheese, this is the place to shop for it: Tons of organic *fromage* is on offer, and most is hormone-free. No wonder people love this place. And truly, it's satisfying to break with social mores and eat at the grocery store: At Whole Foods, it's safe to shop hungry.   ALEX VAN BUREN

WILD
New American, Pizzeria
535 Hudson St. (Perry & Charles St.)
①ⒶⒸⒺⒷⒹⒻⓂ
212 929-2920
eatdrinkwild.com
Mon–Tue: 12pm–10pm,
Wed–Fri: 12pm–11pm,
Sat–Sun: 11am–11pm

Restauranteur Miki Agrawal has revamped her former Slice location in the West Village and is revolutionizing pie standards by using local, seasonal ingredients. Her farm-to-table concept showcases gluten-free rounds with wild yeast crusts and mainly vegan and organic toppings.

Wild's cozy interior features exposed brick, hanging bulbs, and mason jar vases strung along the wall. A small bar serves up craft beer and wine sourced entirely from the Empire state. Fashioned by former Chopped chef Nicholas Porchelli, the menu begins with appetizers like plum tomato and fresh herb bruschetta, a daily soup, and seasonal salads. Hearty kale leaves tossed with smoky tofu cubes, edamame seeds, and olive oil provide a refreshing start. Pizzas are available in personal or share sizes, and a few gluten-free pastas are also offered as main courses.

Thin, crisped, and freshly made every morning, the gluten-free pizza crusts prove to be a sturdy support for the various toppings. Local produce shines in the "Pear Fig Gorgonzola" pie with pear, figs, and fresh rosemary, and the "Skinny Bitch" piles on tender grilled zucchini, sliced eggplant, and cherry tomatoes. Even though the pesto spread was slightly on the oily side, the vibrant flavor made this a great all-veggie option.

Meat lovers have their pick of pies too, like the "Spinach Artichokes" with bacon and goat cheese, or the bold "Spicy Prosciutto" which layers smoked ham and cherry peppers with tangy marinara and melted mozzarella cheese. All of their meats are antibiotic- and hormone-free and carefully sourced from notable area farms.

In addition to lunch and dinner seven days a week, they offer a GF-friendly brunch with specialty housemade cocktails. Whether or not you're accustomed to eating sans gluten, go wild at this impressive downtown café.   MEGAN MURPHY

BAKERIES, ICE CREAMERIES, JUICE BARS

Babycakes
Bakery
248 Broome St. (@ Ludlow)
212 677-5047
babycakesnyc.com

The Butcher's Daughter
Juice Bar
19 Kenmare St.
(Lafayette St. & Cleavland Pl.)
thebutchersdaughter.com

Creative Juice @ Equinox
Multiple Locations (see website)
creativejuiceflows.com

Culture
Ice Creamery
60 W 8th St. (6th Ave & MacDougal St.)
646 823-9715
cultureny.com

Elixir Juice Bar
Multiple Locations (see website)
elixirjuice.com

Elm Health
Juice Bar, Market
1695 First Ave. (@ E. 88th St.)
212 348-8500

56 Seventh Ave. (@ W. 14th St.)
212 255-6300
elmhealth.net

Gingersnap's Organic
Juice Bar, Fast Food
130 E. 7th St. (1st Ave. & Avenue A)
212 533-9939
gingersnapsorganic.com

Great Jones Spa Juice Bar
29 Great Jones St.
(Bowery and Lafayette St.)
212 505-3185
gjspa.com

Green Bean Cafe
Bakery, Juice Bar
1413 York Ave.
(E. 75th & E. 76th St.)
212 861-1539
beangonegreen.com

The Health Nuts
Juice Bar, Market
Multiple Locations (see website)
thehealthnuts.com

Heartbeet Juicery
85 Stanton St
(Orchard St. & Allen St.)
917 338-4646
heartbeetjuicery.com

Jennifer's Way
Bakery
263 E 10th St.
(1st Ave. & Avenue A)
jennifersway.org

Jivamukti Cafe
Juice Bar,
Fast Food
841 Broadway (E. 14th
& E. 13th St.)
212 353-0214
jivamuktiyoga.com

Juice Generation
Multiple Locations
(see website)
juicegeneration.com

The Juice Press
Multiple Locations
(see website)
juicepress.com

Lifethyme
Natural Market
Juice Bar, Market
410 6th Ave. (W. 8th &
W. 9th St.)
212 420-9099
lifethymemarket.com

Liquiteria
Juice Bar
Multiple Locations
(see website)
liquiteria.com

Magic Mix Juicery
102 Fulton St.
(William St. & Dutch
St.)
646 454 0680
magicmixjuicery.com

Melvin's Juice Box
130 W Houston St.
(Sullivan St. &
MacDougal St.)
misslilysnyc.com

Norma Kamali's
Wellness Cafe
Juice Bar,
Fast Food
11 West 56th St.
(5th Ave. & 6th Ave.)
212 957-9797
thewellnesscafe.com

OO Wonder
Juice Bar
265 Columbus Ave
(72nd & 73rd St.)
212 874-0680
oowonder.com

Organic Avenue
Juice Bar
Multiple Locations
(see website)
organicavenue.com

Ronnybrook
Milk Bar
Ice Creamery
75 9th Ave. Chelsea
Market.
(15th and 16th St.)
212 741-6455
ronnybrookmilkbar.
com

Salud
Juice Bar
107 Thompson St.
(Prince St. & Spring St.)
646 398-8615
saludnyc.com

Victory Garden
Ice Creamery
31 Carmine St.
(Bedford St. &
Bleecker St.)
212 206-7273
victorygardennyc.com

Yorganic
Ice Creamery
3 Hanover Sq.
(@ Stone St.)
yorganicnyc.com

INDEX

**Flexitarian Friendly
(good for vegetarians
and carnivores dining
together)**

189